MW00625592

Pull Yourself Up! Pull Yourself Out!

It's Time for A New Level

ISBN 0964659409
Copyright c 2003 by, Reba Haley, Ph.D.
www.RebaHaley.com
Rebahaley2@aol.com
P.O. Box 1034
Valrico, FL 33595

Printed in the United States of America
Unless otherwise indicated, all Scripture are taken
from the King James Version of the Bible.
Library of Congress Cataloging - in Publication
Data Dr. Reba Haley

Life Publishing Company
P.O Box 1034
Valrico, Fl 33595

First edition

CONTENTS

DEDICATION

This book is dedicated to my husband and children and for their love and support.

ACKNOWLEDGEMENT

Thank you God for allowing me to write the book and I pray that it blesses and encourages the reader.

INTRODUCTION

Many of the thoughts in this book were presented in many lectures, counseling sessions and ministerial presentations. My own personal battles with damaged emotions and $100,000 worth of financial debt motivated me to learn how to control, manage my emotions and money. I developed a systematic plan for paying off all my debt and credit cards to bring stability in my financial life. I became a super saver instead of a big spender.

My personal financial storms and burden with debt empowered me to write the book, develop strategies and budgets that will empower you to become debt free. The material presented in the book provides the necessary information to put you on a new financial path.

Honestly, life is not fair and we all have or will have our share of bad breaks. Unavoidable things can happen but you can avoid ruining your financial future.

I made the choice to confront and accept my past emotional hurts and financial mismanagement as I determined to reach stability in both areas. Obtaining my Doctoral Degree in Counseling stemmed from my desire to see other people emotionally, mentally and spiritual healthy. My personal indebtedness led me to secure my Real Estate Broker and Corespondent Mortgage lending licenses to create financial freedom and reach my highest good.

I have dedicated my life to counseling and lecturing people to become financially stable, debt free and emotionally healed. The material contained in the book will give you guidelines to priorities your finances, pay off credit cards, car loans and personal bank loans. This will help you handle your emotions and get out of debt. If you follow the guidelines in the book you will become financially and emotionally stable.

The lack of discipline and knowledge about money creates emotional and financial problems. Financial security will make you feel safe and give you more control over your life. I have counseled many adults with pinned up anger about their financial and emotional problems.

It is important to remember those years of financial mismanagement and damaged emotions will not disappear overnight. Be patience with yourself and apply the guidelines in the book.

God will guide and help you pull yourself up and out. It's time for a new level. God will give you the inner strength and wisdom to make prosperous choices.

Over the years I have learned that healing is a process. Initially I was very impatient. I thought that my quick fix desires to eliminate my emotional pain and repair my financial problems would happen over night. I learned that debt elimination requires a strategy.

Through prayer and understanding the world of money, I began to build and make more money to stay debt free. God wants you debt free and emotionally healthy. Keep in mind that when you follow the guidelines in this book you are on a new financial path.

The Lord placed this book in my heart to help you **Pull Yourself Up! Pull Yourself Out! It's Time for A New Level.**

Chapter 1

Embrace Peace of Mind

I John 4: 18 " There is no fear in love; but perfect love cast out fear because fear is torment. He that feareth is not made perfect in love"

Let go of the fear of your financial past and learn how to handle money. Letting go of the past will give you peace of mind and joy. Fear always distorts our perceptions and confuses us as to what is real. Fear is an emotion and once it takes control of you it will leave you miserable.

Perfect love cast out fear. Where there is love, there is peace. Ultimately, what we all desire is to be loved and have money. However, we're afraid of both. Love means I must be emotionally vulnerable and trust. Financial security requires discipline in spending.

Peace of mind is acquired when we let go of fear and change our behavior. A renewed mind is needed when the old tapes of mistrust, money mismanagement and abandonment play.

It's essential to remember that love is unconditional. We love because God is love and therefore we are able to love and forgive ourselves. Love is the only reality. Love and money goes around and comes around. If you share what you have it might not come back to you from the person that you gave it to, but it will come back around.

If we will, we can use active positive replacement and remove those old tapes and reinforce our love for self through positive affirmation. You can become financially disciplined if you let go of the guilt of the past. We miss love and financial blessings because we won't detach from predictions and control. Therefore, we set our selves up for let downs and misery because we are afraid to trust God in love and finances. We just don't think it can happen to us. Lack of trust in ourselves results in the loss of power. God is love and he will give you a peace of mind and a piece of money.

Fear of the past hinders us from experiencing the present joy. We spend so much time worrying about the future we miss out on living in the here and now. Love is present.

We have free will and can choose to embrace peace and love with money. There is no peace when you are unable to meet your monthly financial obligations. The goal of money is to make you feel secure, give you freedom and grant you more control over your life. There is no lack of money in the world. The love of universe God is vast and His ways are not our ways. If you open your mind too new ideals and thoughts God will supplement your income and increase your finances. You are the author of your life.

Using negative words such as can't and impossible impose limits and replays those old fearful tapes. Obtaining and maintaining peace of mind is the single goal. We must make a conscious decision to follow peace if we want to have peace.

The key for peace is forgiveness and self-fulfillment. To forgive someone is not about them. It's the reality for your peace of mind. Some people have unlovable behavior. However, God commands that you and I love the person. You cannot allow the things that people say or their behavior to define your life and hinder you from reaching your financial goals.

People do not determine your life. They do not have to change for you to reach your goals and acquire peace of mind. Do what is right for you first and then take care of other people.

Our present perceptions are developed by our past encounters. However, if those encounters were unhealthy then our perception is distorted.

To experience total financial freedom and embrace peace you must be honest with yourself, relinquish negative self-defeating words and share with other people.

The first and most important thing is for you to become a giver. Money is for movement and circulation. If you want money to come back to you, you must first release it into the universe. Your spirit and your happiness are far more important than your money.

Money can help you feel safe, protected and happy. Becoming financially stable requires discipline in your spending and a new way of thinking. In order to embrace peace of mind it is necessary to shift our thinking. Love is the only reality and anything else is a thief to peace.

Embracing peace of mind comes with not wanting to control other people. Inner peace can be reached only when we allow people the freedom to be who they are without bigotry.

Money should not be used as the thermostat to gauge our success. Success is more than money.

God has provided everything that we need and it's within us. The peace of mind and financial freedom are internally processed. External things are temporal but peace of mind and debt elimination is internally motivated.

You must determine what your needs are and what you want. If we base the things we want on another person we will love them when we get it and we will hate them when we don't get what we think we want.

Obtaining money or material possession by lying and manipulation opens a window to financial loss. Money obtained in truth will generate wealth. However, changing the old belief and methods of securing objects in this manner require that your mind be changed to embrace peace. Believe that what God has for you will come to you. Most successful people decide what they want out of life and make it a priority.

A new thought pattern and behavioral change will increase your finances. Words can build or tear down a person's motivation and self-esteem. It's important always to be gentle with people as we communicate and become people of peace.

In our families, marriages and with our loved ones choose love rather than anger, resentment, hostility and bitterness. I learned that in a marriage relationship, we must allow our marital partners some liberty. A good marriage is built on shared values, with both people pulling financially in the same direction.

Communication will rid us of fear and financial problems. Marital couples with incomes can develop a goal of financial freedom and accomplish it in a short time.

Our society has lost the value of family, love and concern for others. Christians attend church on Sundays, hear the message of tithing and giving but they do not apply the principles. People express their love for God but there is no love for their neighbor.

Violence, anger, backbiting, political division, church denominational separation and racism divides us all. We say America is one nation under God. Is God divided?

Truthful communication about financial matters and stewardship will promote financial prosperity and peace in our country, churches and homes.

Most marriages end in divorce over the lack of finances or money mismanagement. Why? Most couples don't seriously discuss money until after they are married.

The number of divorced and never married adults increased says Census Bureau Report. Between 1970 and 1996, the number of divorced persons has more that quadrupled, from 4.3 million to 18.3 million. The number of never married adults has more than doubled, from 21.4 million to 44.9 million, reported by the Commerce Department.

This report includes these highlights:

-   The median age for first marriages has risen from the age of 19.5 to 24.8 years for women and 27.1 years for men in 1996.

-   Between 1970 and 2001 , the proposition of 18 – to 24 years old who family household or their spouses decreased from 38 percent to 20 percent for 25 to 34 years olds the proposition decreased from 83 percent to 61 percents.

- Between 1970 and 2001 the proposition of children under 18 years of age living with one parent grew from 12 percent to 28.

- The number of unmarried couple household (couples of opposite sexes) grew from 523,000 in 1970 to 4 million.

The latest divorce statistic from Georgia Barna is sobering. One quarter of all Americans have experienced at least one divorce. Born again Christians continue to have a higher likelihood of getting divorced than do non- Christians. Atheists are less likely to get divorced than are born again Christians. These are just some of the statistic from his latest insight into divorce. Divorce has gone from rare to routine within a generation.

George Barna concludes that "divorce may not be popular, but it remains common in America"

The President of the United States has proposed a bill to encourage marriage among single women receiving government assistance. What a dramatic change in society's marital views.

The statistic is bothersome. Christians should be setting the example. The church is represented as the bride and Jesus the bridegroom. Marriage is biblically represented as Christ and the Church. Instead, Christian marriages appear to be no different than those in the world who do not represent themselves as Christians.

Not long ago Christians talked about the low divorce rates among Christians as evident of how God and Christian faith can provide a firm foundation for marriage. This is not true today.

The divorce rate is so alarming that various States have implemented a 3-day waiting period prior to getting married. Other states are requiring potential marital license applicants to watch a video.

In counseling married couples, I have discovered that marriages end in divorce for a variety of reasons: They have out grown one another in interest, married when they were very young and no longer feel the same way towards the other spouse. Adultery, financial, sexual, physical and verbal abuse are also reasons people seek divorce.

It's important to embrace peace of mind in every situation and decision. Be prepared to give an account to the love of the universe God for your thoughts and decisions.

It's your mind and your choice. I think that marriage is worth working through issues. I encourage martial couples to attend marriage counseling and conferences that provide a blueprint and insight for building a successful marriage.

By consciously and consistently choosing love rather than fear we will embrace peace of mind and experience joy. Let's keep our minds stayed on the love of the universe God and change our financial behavior. If we practice changing our behavior and keep focused we will encounter financial security. Facing the truth and acquiring the necessary financial skills limit the mistakes we are likely to make. The price of mistakes is costly and can be eliminated or limited by seeking wisdom and counsel. It's okay to be ignorant; however it's not okay to stay ignorant.

Financial knowledge is readily available and accessible. If we ask, seek and knock the information will be given. If you have a vision that is God breathed you will have provision. When we ask the love of the universe God for things and make our request known to Him we must have faith in him. Faith will produce prosperity and peace. Remember, when request, are made known God will answer yes, no or not now.

Accepting Gods responses to our request exemplifies growth and maturity. We realize that God would keep his promises and supply the needs.

Remember if His answer is not now that does not mean ever. Trust is the first step to spiritual maturity.

It would benefit you greatly to establish a personal relationship with God as Father and receive the wisdom that comes from Him. He said, " No good thing will I withhold from them that walk uprightly before me". If God is your Father then you can trust him to provide and meet your needs on time.

Spoken words of faith will produce peace of mind. If you struggle with issues of distrust it comes from the lack of faith. Possibly, your parents failed you as a child and you concluded as an adult that God would fail you. Realize that as children of God we have been adopted. His knowledge, wisdom and love illuminates from Heaven and is shared in our hearts.

He can be trusted and His divine plan will be revealed in our lives. God has given you and I wisdom to survive thus far and we shall be financially successful and have peace in this world. There are ideas and things that God has told and visions He has shown you.

Peace and patience will bring those things too past. God saw your tears and heard your cry to Him at night, while you laid on your bed all alone, asking Him, why me? The lord is not slack concerning his promises.

Patience is truly powerful and will create what you need and allow you to keep what you have. Patience will develop discipline and build character, in time. So often we share our visions and dreams with other people and expect them to be glad and inspirational.

Unfortunately, the majority of people will not support or encourage your dreams or ideas. Accept their opinions, but don't base your value as a person on their rejection. Don't make their opinion your reality. In fact, it is your reality and responsibility to fulfill the dreams and visions that are in our heart.

It is your responsibility to become financially responsible and acquire money management skills to feel safe and financially protected. You are responsible for your own destiny and the world is waiting on you to make a difference. Your dreams and visions require money. If we don't have money you can't pay your bills or fulfill your vision. No money, no peace.

The love of the universe God put the vision in your heart. Have faith and develop a written business plan to produce the ideal and vision. Those ideals can produce wealth and provide financial freedom. Mary told the disciples "Just do what Jesus (God) tells you to do". You will experience jealously, envy and strife from other men and women who are insecure in their own inability and choose not to succeed.

These people will literally hate you for you ability to endure and fulfill your set goals and desires without their assistance.

 Negative people will say, " You can't do this", or "You can't have that", as you share your ideas and dreams with them. Release those negative people. Choose to be your own friend and take care of your financial and emotional needs.

Success will be achieved as you apply goals to your dreams, visions and ideals. Pray to receive financial freedom and peace.

Chapter 2

Healing Damaged Emotions

Many people are hurting and crying out for help to be healed of damaged emotions. Healing is acquired by asking the love of the universe God for healing. God will not withhold anything good from those that live righteous. Healing rises above pain and receives relief.

You must believe by faith that the love of the universe God is able, willing and desires to see you healed. "Perfect love cast out fear." Doubt will inhibit your healing. Your words will cause sickness or healing to come into your life.

Emotional pain is felt and usually fear produces pain. To change we must feel and attempt to find the root cause of the pain. Perhaps, as a child you grew up being verbally abused, ignored, neglected and was told that you were ugly.

Possibly, during your childhood you missed an opportunity to connect with your true self and develop your self-image. Thereafter, a negative self-image was developed.

Allow yourself permission to feel grief and grow through the pain of the past. My desire to see other people emotionally and spiritually healthy motivated me to attend college and obtain a Master of Science Degree in Psychology and Doctoral Degree in Counseling. In counseling persons with addictions or who have addicted loved ones, I suggest they attend the various 12 step group meeting such as Adult Children of Alcoholics, Alcoholic for Christ, Al Anon, Alcoholic Anonymous (AA) and Alateen for children aids in the healing process.

In an attempt to help families work through their issues these groups provide support. Hurting people need a place that identifies with the pain and shame of their addictions, addicted loved ones or children that were victims of abuse.

These groups provide support and establish a family within themselves. Emotional healing is a process and can not take place overnight. It's one day at a time.

The 12 step program is a spiritual program and not religious by nature. These steps provide a structure and spiritual enlightenment that allows the love of the universe God to provide the answers and give strength to make the necessary choices.

These groups provide sponsors that are seniors in the 12-step program who provide support for you as you work through your issues and attend the meeting.

It's a misnomer that religious is the only cure for healing of damaged emotions. Counseling, 12 step programs, reading the bible and prayer can aid in the spiritual recovery and healing of damaged emotions. As a born Christian in my early formative years I frequented the Adult Children of Alcoholics meeting to break several dysfunctional patterns. Through prayer and meditation I became emotionally and spiritually healthier. However, everyone who attends these meetings and counseling does not want to get well. Facing truth was the key that brought healing in my life.

I grew up an Adult Child of an Alcoholic and had some childhood hurts and learned some unhealthy behaviors that lead me into unhealthy relation-ships. After several dysfunctional and unhealthy interpersonal relationships, I attended the 12-step meeting and secured a sponsor. The message from my sponsor was, "if you don't get some help you will continue to gravitate and select needy people that are emotionally unavailable" and she said, " attend the meeting for one year and don't enter into any intimate relationships."

The dysfunctional cycle was broken as I adhered to my sponsor's suggestions. I began to self-care and became honest with my feelings about my past. Trying to please other people and take care of them was my problem. I neglected my own desires and feelings as I sought to please other people. Healing came in my life as I worked through my pain and the unresolved issues in my life. I was an emotional mess. It took God to heal me of my past emotional wounds.

I stop blaming my parents, the past and the system for my pain. I realized that life held similar to a card game and I began to play the hand that I had been dealt. As children, you and I were born to parents and lived in cities that we did not choose. Life dealt us a hand that we had no choice in. I hear children growing up saying," I have fears and resent being born a person of color, or Hispanic". This verbal communication is heard within their family of origin regarding the lack of visual observations of minorities and people of color in commercial advertisement, media personnel and other professions. The lack of visual cultural diversity displayed in various media outlets reinforces their fears.

The media reflects images in the United States of America that the nation is predominately composed of only one race.

Our society should increase visual diversity and incorporate people of all races in various professions. Our children are the future and this will build their self-esteem and together they can build a unified country. Our churches can reinforce diversity and communicate that God created people in different nationalities. God knows and does what is best in the lives of individuals.

Regardless of your color, nationality or past life there is no system or person that can stop you from achieving your desired goals. If God be for you, who can be against you?

Healing from the old negative tapes first starts with knowing who you are in God and pressing forward to reach your goals. Play the hand you've been dealt and play to win.

If you have addicted loved ones you will have debt due to their substance abuse consummation. If you have an addiction or addicted loved ones, I recommend that you attend one of the 12 step groups. Alcoholic Anonymous, Adult Children of Alcoholic, Al Anon and Alateen provides support in group format for loved ones, addicts or alcoholics supporting persons seeking strength, and hope to solve their common problems.

12 STEP PROGRAM

1. We admitted we were powerless over alcohol that our lives had become unmanageable.

2. Came to believe that a Power greater than ourselves could restore us to sanity.

3. Made a decision to turn our will and our lives over to the care of God, as we understood Him.

4. Made a searching and fearless moral inventory of ourselves.

5. Admitted to God, to ourselves, and to another human being the exact nature of our wrongs.

6. Were entirely ready to have God remove all these defects of character.

7. Humbly asked Him to remove our shortcomings.

8. Made a list of all person we had harmed, and became willing to make amends to them all.

9. Made direct amends to such people wherever possible, expect when to do so would injure them or others.

10. Continued to take personal inventory and when we were wrong promptly admitted it.

11. Sought through prayer and mediation to improve our conscious contact with God, as we understood him, praying only for knowledge of his will for us and the power to carry that out.

12. Having had a spiritual awakening as the result of these Steps, we tired to carry this message to others, and to practice these principles in all our affairs.

Alateen is a support 12 step group for teens that have parents with addictions. This group helps children realize (5) five things:

1. They are not alone in having an addicted or abusive parent.
2. They can't control their parent's addiction or abuse.
3. They didn't cause the addiction or abuse
4. They can't do anything to cure the addiction or abuse.
5. They can live happy beyond the addiction or abuse.

This provides freedom from guilt for teens when they realize those 5 simple things. Alateen provides prevention that helps teens become emotionally and spiritually healthy adults.

Al Anon Family group is for families and friends of alcoholics. The group provides support for family members who have loved ones that are alcoholics or drug addicts.

Al Anon Family group supports:

1. Teach you how to emotionally detach from addicted loved ones.
2. Focus on helping to provide support for the addicted love one.
3. Supports the discontinuous of enabling the loved one.
4. Weekly group support meetings.
5. Sponsors

Alcoholic Anonymous is a fellowship of men and women who share their experiences, strength and hope with each other that they may solve their common problem and help others to recover from alcoholism.

They provide support:

1. Helps the alcoholic not to drink.
2. Provide supports during their withdraw from alcoholism.
3. Weekly group supports meetings.
4. Achieve sobriety through talking and support.

Adult Children of Alcoholics (ACOA) is a group of adult children that grew up in alcoholic homes and were subjected to unhealthy behavior in their family of origin.

ACOA provides support:

1.   Weekly support meeting.
2.   Work through unhealthy behavioral issues.
3.   Group support during behavioral changes.

The serenity prayer is repeated during every meeting. "God Grant me the serenity to accept the things and people that I cannot change, courage to change the things that I can and wisdom to know the difference."

These groups are spiritual in nature and promote emotional and spiritual healing.

Chapter 3

Healing the Abused Child

According to the 1994 survey of the Child Abuse and Neglect Statistics from the National Committee to Prevent Child Abuse. Physical abuse represented 21% of confirmed cases, sexual abuses 11%, neglect 49%, emotional maltreatment 3% and other forms of maltreatment 16%. These percentages have remained fairly stable since 1986 when approximately 27% of the children were reported abused, 16% for sexual abuse, 55% for neglect, and 8% for emotional maltreatment (AAPC, 1988). In the year 2000, about 3 million American families (5 million kids) were referred to child protection agencies. Less than 2 million of those referrals resulted in investigation. Findings of abuse /neglect were made on about ½ of those families (879,000 children)

In other words while 879,000 children were found to be in need of service, about 4 million children had to endure strip searches, interrogations and home inspection for nothing. Of the 879,000 found to be allegedly maltreated 568,000, were in foster care. What happen to family preservation?

This is why ALL the states are completely OUT OF COMPLIANCE with ASFA 97 because they aren't even pretending to reunify families once they have torn them up.

This is a very accurate account statistic and statement regarding all States.

In Interim FY 2000

- 47% lived with foster families who are not related to them
- 25% lived with relatives who are their foster parents
- 4% lived in pre-adoptive homes
- 8% lived in group homes
- 10% lived in institutions
- 1% were in supervised independent living arrangements
- Approximately 2% were runaways
- 3% were on trial visits homes with their parents

47% of abused children are snatched from their homes, placed in foster care and in the homes of strangers. Usually these children come to a foster home with only the clothes they are wearing.

Usually, these children receive no counseling. If counseling is provided it is 2 or 3 years after they have been in foster care. Foster parents are paid monthly to provide shelter for children in foster care.

I have been a foster mother for 4 years providing shelter, clothes, love and support for abused children. I sought divine guidance and became a foster mother. During that time I rationalized the thought of becoming a foster mother with the fact that I had a big house and needed to give something back to society.

Understand that as a child I lived in several foster homes. God placed this desire in my heart to care for abused and neglected children, as life events came full circle. During my teenage years I grew up in a home where my mother had a nervous breakdown and my father became a functional alcoholic. The term functional alcoholic is defined as one who maintains a job but drinks daily. My mother was a housewife who stayed home. My father showed me love and attention, as I was the first born of two and the only girl. My father's alcohol drinking progressed and led to my parent's divorce. I was a very angry, hurt and rebellious teenager.

My mother's sister took me and sibling brother into her home after my father left and my mother was placed in a State Mental Hospital. The weekly visitation to the mental hospital depressed me and made me angry. At the age of 15 I ran away from my aunt's home to stay with friends. However, that didn't last long. Their parents put me out and the police picked me up as a missing person who was truant from school. Well, I found myself in the Youth Home Detention Center where I stayed and was placed in two foster homes.

Miss Brown's foster home was the first home where I lived. She was a mean and angry woman. She was a foster mother who was concerned only with supplementing her income and receiving a check from the foster care agency. I felt very uncomfortable and unwanted and asked the social worker to move me into another foster home, and she did.

Thereafter, I went to Mr. and Mrs. White's foster home. They were Christian foster parents and church attendees. I had my own room, they took me to church, bought me clothes, showed me compassion and love.

I became a foster mother to help abused children because of my personal experience and it was important to me to provide a loving and safe home for the children living in foster home. I have taken into my home over (25) twenty-five children, (6) six at a time, over a 4-year period. God had given me great opportunity to share love and invest in the lives of children.

Let me share with you a great story about a little girl whose name we shall call Kim. Kim came to live with us at the of age 6. She had no clothes, her hair was matted and smelled deplorable. Kim had never been to school in her life. She lived in the streets, had not bathed in months and ate out of garbage cans with her mother. Kim's mother was a schizophrenic and Kim's grandmother was also mentally ill.

Investing in Kim's life and education proved to be very rewarding for Kim, as well as myself. I was a college graduate and professor; therefore I was equipped to help Kim with her education. I enrolled Kim in Elementary school in Kindergarten at age 7. She went to 1st grade at age 8 and at age 8 she was went to 2nd grade. She worked so hard and was promoted to 3rd grade at the age of 9. At age 10 she was in the 4th grade and at age 11 she went to the 5th grade. Now she was in the age appropriate grade level.

A very true and great success story! It is very rewarding investing in the life of a child. My home provided a safe and stable haven for these children as they went through life's transition. I asked Kim. "What do you want to be.?" She said, "I want to go to college and teach like you".

We all can make a difference in the lives of children.

Kim was brought into my life and home by the love of the universe God. Therefore, I decided to do something very special for Kim. So, I took my daughter and Kim on a 5-day cruise to Mexico. We arrived at the ship and they said, "let's get a hotdog". I said, "Okay." We went to the hot dog stand outside the port and got several hot dogs. As we were leaving the man inside the hot dog stand said, "Bye Kim."

I turned back around and said, "Excuse me?" "How do you know her name?" The man said." I am her father." I looked at Kim and said, "Is this your father?" She said, "Yes. " I said, "What is his name?" She said, "Ron". The man said. "That's my name". Ron came from inside the hot dog stand and kissed his daughter as we all cried. Kim had not seen her father since she was 4 years old and at that time she was 9 years old.

The foster care agency claimed they had been searching for her father for 5 years. With divine intervention from the love of the universe God, Kim reunited with her biological father.

During Kim's stay, I took her to church, she went to the opera, Disney World, Universal Studios, Island of Adventure, horse backing riding, and she learned how to swim. I taught her to cook, clean, iron, wash her clothes and count her money.
I wanted to make sure that when she left my home, she would be able to take care of her self. I reminded her often to continue to pray and respect her mother in her sickness.

Becoming a foster mother has been a rewarding and spiritual experience, and changed my life.

Love is the real healer for children of abuse. Love demonstrated in a child's life will change their life forever. You and I encounter children everyday and we have an opportunity by the love of the universe God to impact and influence their lives.

Whenever we encounter a child, let's make the relationship loving and memorable as you become energy of love. Children are our future!

Those abused and homeless children who came into my home were not my children; but they are the future. I encourage everyone that has a heart for children to consider becoming a foster parent and make a difference in the life of a child.

There are thousands of children in foster care that need loving homes and stable people to love them as they go through life's' transitions. Abused and neglected children in foster care are victims and need you to share your love with them.

I recommend when you become a foster parent that you give your immediate family and children individual attention. Separate and respite time away from the foster children is encouraged to strengthen and maintain the emotional bond with your children and spouse.

Foster fathers play an important role in the life of foster children. Most of the children in foster care have grown up in a single female head of household home. As a man, this is a great opportunity to be a role model and share in the life of a child.

If you decide to become a foster father, remember God has placed men as the head, of their homes as He did Adam.

Adam was given complete instruction by God to cultivate, guard and bear fruit in the earth. Prior to Adam disobeying the love of the universe God, he was morally innocent.

Disobedience caused Adam to lose his spiritual connection, separated Him from the love of universe God and diminished his spiritual hearing. The loves of the universe God instructions are clear. The man is the head of the house. Males are born, men are developed and fathers are created.

If as a man you are not where you should be positionally, God can give you the wisdom to lead your family into blessings and peace. This will equip you to lead foster children to God, bring healing to abused children and members of your family.

The statistics of abused children are straggling. The U.S Department of Health and Human Services released a survey that showed the number of abused and neglected children increased from 1.4 millions in 1986 to over 2.8 million in 1993 nearly doubling in seven years. The number of children who were seriously injured quadrupled from about 143,000 nearly 570,000.

If you're a man perhaps you have been in relationships with women who emotionally, physically abused, neglected and abandoned you. If this is your situation, the love of the universe God wants you healed of your past hurts from women that have come into your life. You do not have to pretend that those relationships did not hurt you and portray an image of emotional strength. Realize that you were wounded and bruised from those relationships with women. "Let the weak say, I am strong." Joel 3:10

This scripture is not intended to imply that you must be strong, but you must confess to possess strength.

God will bring emotional healing and as you pray and patiently wait on the love of your life, God will lead you to find your wife.

Forgiveness and letting go of the past promotes emotional healing. Lay aside resentment, bitterness and anger regarding the things that happened or the people who hurt you. Negative thoughts only hurt you and inhibit you from experiencing all the wonderful things that God has for you. If you don't relinquish the resentment and anger it will transfer to the women in your life, if you don't let them go.

Thereafter, you will marry only to divorce Sue, marry Ann, only to later divorce Ann and later marry Jane. The cycle will repeat itself. Without counseling and spiritual intervention, these women in your life become victims and emotionally abused by being in a relationship with you.

The emotions of fear, rejection and abandonment need to be confronted. Honestly confronting these feelings will help you to open up and learn to give as well as receive love.

When you have honestly confronted those fears you will be able to establish emotionally healthy relationships with women.

Men are very special in the eyes of the creator God and He wants the best for you. God commands that we love one another. Men need to see and meet other men that are committed to God, impacting their communities and are faithful spouses. The prisons are full of men that have been abused as children and seek to find the healing and peace in God.

My academic achievements and work experience in counseling, granted me an opportunity for (8) eight years to provide didactic lectures to incarcerated men and women who were charged with drug related offenses.

These inmates were court ordered to attend the in jail substance abuse treatment program. Approximately 31% of women in Prison state they had been abused as children, according to the United States Department of Justice. Long term effects of child abuse include fear, anxiety, depression, anger, hostility, inappropriate sexual behavior, poor self-esteem, and tendency towards substance abuse and difficulty with close relationships.

A clinical finding of adult victims of sexual abuse includes problems with interpersonal relationships associated with an underlying mistrust.

Generally, adult victims of incest have a severely estranged relationship with their parents that are marked by feelings of mistrust, fear, ambivalence, hatred, and betrayal. These feelings may extend to all family members. (Tsai and Wagner,)

Early identification of sexual abuse victims appears to be crucial to the reduction of suffering of abused youth. Establishment of support systems for assistance in pursuing appropriate psychological and spiritual counseling produces healthy adult functioning. As long as secrecy continues to be a proven for young victims, fear, suffering and mental distress will like secrecy remain with the victims. Pinned up anger can result in violent criminal activities.

According to The Associated Press women now make up a bigger slice of all those arrested in the United States, according to the 2003 FBI Report. Arrests of men and women in 2002 are part of the FBI annual look at serious crime. It found a slight increase of less than one-tenth of 1 percent to about 11.9 million murders, rapes, theft, robberies, burglaries, aggravated assault and vehicle theft.

Men still account for the vast majority of adults arrested for these and other crimes, about 77 percent. Women are gaining ground, with 1.9 million arrested in 2002 making up 23 percent. That is a 14 percent increase from 1993, a period which arrests of men have fallen almost 6 percent.

An even larger jump occurred between 1986 and 1995 when arrest of women rose by almost 38%.

Between 1993 and 2002, women's arrest for murder, robbery, burglary, theft and arson fell. Increases for women were most dramatic for such crimes as embezzlement (80 percent), forgery and counterfeiting (19 percent), drug abuse (50 percent) vagrancy (42 percent) and liquor law violations (49 percent).

Kenneth Land, a professor of sociology at Duke University, attributed the rise in female arrest to societal changes over the past 30 years.

More women have entered the work force and generally have achieved a status on a par with men. "You're more likely to have situations where they can be involved as motivated offenders due to the role changes over the past decade, as compared to men." Land said.

Without the healing of the love of the universe God, victimized women become criminals. There is hope in the love of the universe God. He desires women to aspire and be spiritually healed from child abuse and past hurts. Emotionally healing helps you become a woman of virtue. Counseling women and providing spiritual enlightenments have proven effective as they reflect back to their Christian and spiritual roots to ignite the healing process.

If a child is reared in a home with spiritual teaching that child as an adult will draw from those encounters. Prior to my mother's illness she would take us to church and there I spent my early formative years. At the age of (12) twelve, my Christian mother led me to Christ and I became born again. I had the great opportunity in church to grow up around older seasoned women of God.

We went to church every Sunday morning and night, Wednesday and Friday nights.

As I look back on my life and church attendance, it is clear that my mother was seeking peace in her life. She found peace in the church, prayer and reading her bible. Due to her illness my mother, didn't teach me things that a young lady should know but she introduced me to the love of the universe Jesus.

These seasoned older women in the church would pray with me on Friday nights, during intercessory prayer meeting. They would tell me "Baby if you don't learn nothing else, we're to teach you how to pray." These women would spend hours and hours crying out as we kneeled at the chair and called on the name of Jesus. They would call him Master, Keeper, Redeemer, Lord and the only true and living God. They would pray until the glory of the Lord would fill that Pentecostal Church. These seasoned older women taught me to dress modest and think pure thoughts. They taught me to live a righteous and morally upright life. This has spiritually strengthened me as an adult today.

I established a personal relationship with God as Father at an early age. My earthly father was an alcoholic. His alcohol consummation increased and he lost his job at the automotive factory. He lost focus on self, family and was consumed with drinking.

My father was later diagnosed with cancer and died. During his alcoholic drinking he was unable to give our family the love that it needed to remain whole. I began to seek the face of God as my Father. In my mind I viewed God as my Father who cared and would provide for me.

I thought and believed that if I were a good girl, that our Heavenly Father would love and heal the pain in my heart. I later learned that God's love is unconditional and we can not ever be good enough to earn His love.

I also knew that I had experienced a lot of pain in my life; therefore, I had no choice but to love and believe that God would reveal his plan for my life and heal my pain. Out of pain and desperation, I clung to Gods word for dear life.

Through prayer I began to seek a female role model. I was lead to read about the different women in the bible and admired Queen Esther.

1. **How she sought divine guidance in difficult times. Esther 4:15-17**
2. **How she renounced herself for the sake of others.**
3. **To value and seek the cooperation from other believers.**

Queen Esther was strong-minded, clear on judgment, illustrated magnificent self-control and was capable to noble self-sacrifice.

Proverbs 31: 10, "Who can find a virtuous woman? For her price is far above rubies."

10 Keys to become a Virtuous Woman

1. Commitment to obeying the word of God.
2. Meek and quiet spirit.
3. Adorning ones spirit with worship and praise.
4. A heart and mouth full of wisdom.
5. Possess the gift of discernment.
6. Economic and financial awareness.
7. Concerned about the affairs of others.
8. Love and devotion for your husband and family.
9. Have a heart for the poor.
10. Produce wealth with your hands and abilities.

God does not require that you and I are perfect. The love of the universe God wants us to have faith in His ability to pull us out of emotional pain and financial troubles.

Chapter 4

Spiritual Restoration

"Brethren, if a man be overtaken in a fault, ye which are spiritual restore such an one in the spirit of meekness; considering thyself lest thou also be tempted." Galatians 6: 1

Agape is unconditional love that is shown to us by the love of the universe God in offering His only begotten Son to die on the cross for you and I. We didn't deserve for Jesus to lay down His life and die a sinner's death for us. God gave us His love, Jesus that we might believe on Him and not perish but have everlasting life. The love of the universe God wants us to know Him, share our faith and His love with others.

The church has taught Christians how to have faith in God to obtain material possession and things. Christians drive luxury cars, have careers, wear the latest fashions, wear false fingernails, gloried hair and their children attend private schools. There are millions of Christian people attending church religiously every Sunday.

The majority of attendees are not committed to sharing His love and impacting their communities. Love in action will be openly seen and draw people to itself. Love produces an attitude of gratitude. Therefore, if you have a job and income that is meeting your families' financial needs, you are blessed!

If you have a job, God gave you that job. If you have completed your college degree, God gave you that degree. The skills that we have acquired should be used to promote God's agenda. His agenda is to seek and save those who are lost and share His love.

Honestly, everything that is good comes from God. Without God, the love of the universe, you and I are nothing. Therefore, we should share the hope in God and love with others.

Once I accepted Jesus and made Him Lord of my life I spiritually matured and found my reason for living. Purpose in life is to share His love, encourage and inspire other people to do the will of God the Father.

Sharing positive words can rebuild relationships and remove years of guilt from the past. Love is the only reality. Always be gentle with yourself and others.

Practice eliminating self-defeating words and negative thoughts. Replace those negative words and thoughts with positive ones and avoid judging others. Some people are judgmental and concentrate on everyone else's mistakes and faults without looking at themselves. Perhaps, you were brought up in a home where you heard negative criticism and your faults were constantly discussed, emotional healing of your past will enable you to spiritually restore others.

Remember that the goal is to spiritually restore others in the spirit of meekness and in love. Judging and faultfinding others are not characteristic of love and will not heal damaged emotions. Mending the broken hearted and spiritually restoring others is promoted by loving others and not judging.

Love is the only reality and it can be easier to concentrate on the strength of others and look over their faults. This means that we see others in a loving way, as we want others to see us. Not judging others requires letting go of fear and embrace the love of others. The love of the universe God teaches us to accept people as they are until they decide to change.

During their process we are simultaneously learning to accept our faults and love ourselves. Reserving judgment of others frees us from being judged by others. If you sow judgement in the lives of others you will receive judgement. What you sow is what you shall reap!

Learn not to make condemning judgements against anyone. Be willing to extend love and mercy to everyone that you meet. God has given us a commandment that we love one another. Some people think that they are better than someone else possibly, because they are not divorced, have not had children out of wedlock, never been addicted to drugs or alcohol or have children on drugs.

If these things have not happened to you it's only by the grace of God! You are not exempt and neither are your children from the negative influences in this world. God wants us to be kind and show patience towards other people. As, we consider ourselves less we become as they are or be in their situation.

Spiritual restoration requires the development of listening skills. We need to hear what the other person is saying without completing their sentence for them. It's rude to talk when someone else is talking.

If you are talking when someone is talking this inhibits you from hearing what he or she is saying. This requires self control (temperance). People who interrupt others while they are talking aren't really concerned with what the other person is saying. They are only concerned with making their point.

Spiritually restoring others require that we listen to what they are saying and not to what we want or think they are saying. First, repeat the question back to the person to ensure that you have accurately heard what the person said. Next, confirm what you heard by repeating it back to them. Be quick to listen, slow to speak and slow to anger. To ensure that you have understood the person correctly it would be nice to get an understanding prior to ending the conversation.

The United States of America has a cultural mixture of people with diverse languages and beliefs. It would be beneficial to ascertain an understanding in communication as to why people believe like they believe. Perhaps, it may differ from your opinion.

However, the restoration of others requires that we open our minds and be subjective in our views. As we become older our hearing and understanding diminishes.

Also, some have a tendency to reflect and project their past biases, ideals, thoughts and learned behaviors on others. Thereafter, we become impatient and intolerant of other people and their problems. Due to the lack of patience and tolerance of others, some are seeking less religious and more spiritual people to connect with. Families need to be spiritually healed so they can spiritually strengthen others.

So often we become involved in everyone else's problems that we don't focus on helping our immediate family. However, there is nothing more important than your family.

I have counseled many businessmen, women and Minister's attempting to save the world and achieve their financial goals while traveling the world only to lose their family in the process.

Unfortunately, we have placed church, jobs, people and everything else before our families only to find that our children are on drugs and husbands or wives are having adulterous affairs. First, we must prioritize our lives and realize our families are first. When the family is truly happy they can provide spiritual restoration to others. The love of the universe God wants us to bond and spend time together as a family to create a spiritual and harmonious relationship among one another.

Secondly, we must become spiritual before we can spiritually restore anyone else. This requires reading the Bible to find certain scriptures of healing and faith.

Thirdly, we need to mediate and prepare our spirits to receive instructions from the love of the universe God. Finally, we must ensure that the timing to share the instruction is appropriate.

Love is the only reality. Wisdom is the principal thing and let us embrace, peace, love and pull others up and out of emotional bondage. The love of the universe God will give you instructions for others as well as for yourself. He speaks in dreams, visions, audibly and through the Bible. The love of the universe God will never give you a word differing from His written word.

Therefore, it would be beneficial to confirm the heard word with the written word in the Bible.

Habakkuk 2: 2-4 " Write the vision, and make it plain upon tables, that he may run that readeth it. For the vision is yet for an appointed time, but at the end it shall speak and not lie: though it tarry, wait for it; because it will surely come, it will not tarry."

Writing down your ideas, visions and dreams is the first step to bringing them to fruition. I believe what you believe and desire, will manifest in time. Sometimes, we move a head of God in an attempt to perform the task without seeking spiritual guidance.

On occasion we all have made mistakes, missed the mark and moved ahead of God with the vision. God will give you wisdom, instructions and guidance on how to fulfill the ideas, visions and the desires that are in your heart.

Our society stands in desperate need for more of God, moral discipline to maintain the blessing of God and keep our nation safe. We can't say we love God and hate people. Good works cannot produce righteousness. We can never be good enough or work hard enough to obtain righteousness.

Righteousness is a gift from the love of the universe God. *Proverb 14: 34 "Righteousness exalts a nation: but sin is a reproach to any people"*. Individual behavior is directly related to ones thoughts. Your mind must be renewed as you attempt to spiritually restore others.

Freedom in your mind will loose you from racism, anger, hatred, complacency, tradition and idolatry, which will enable you to spiritually restore others.

The White House, your house or my house will not stand and be victorious until we set the goal to work together for the betterment of one another. The spirit to agree will ensure peace and success within our homes, jobs, and communities and in our country. It is wisdom to seek after peace in all relationships and to find a middle ground to agree upon.

Aspire to set goals to arrive at a peaceful outcome. The power of agreement will allow us to experience peace and build character in our lives and in the lives of others.

Humbleness in action means that you and I don't have to be right. You can be wrong and still be happy. Perhaps, you find yourselves arguing about who's right or whose point is right and miss the purpose of the discussion. At that point you are perplexed and must reflect back to the original discussion, to find out what the current discussion is really all about.

During the current discussion or argument one finds they rehash issues that have been previously discussed and/ or resolved.

Repetitive discussions about the past will hinder the growth for the future. You can not keep looking back, embracing old baggage and expect to spiritually restore others and experience a life of peace.

A perpetual relationship established with the love of the universe God through prayer, meditation and worship will create peace within and equip you to spiritually restore others. The love of the universe God wants to give you His heart as you embrace His word and seek His spiritual guidance. The spirit of God will give you a heart that desires to see other people blessed.

He will give a heart of love, courage and spiritually lead you to engage in a conversation with a total stranger. Once engaged in that conversation you may find that the person had a message for you. Therefore, you can't be afraid to approach people that are different from you. That person might be holding your blessing.

If you are a believer, Christianity does not require that you and I are perfect but that we're committed to loving others and maintaining peace.

God uses people that are spiritually filled with His love to pull others up and out of their emotional pain.

Chapter 5

Live Beyond the Past

The original plan of God for marriage was to produce godly offspring. However, sin began with the first family, Adam and his wife, Eve. Eve conceived and bore Cain and Abel. Cain killed his brother, then lied to God about the murder. Genesis 4:1-9 Sin originated in the first family and continues on today.

All humanity experience or possess some level of dysfunction in their family of origin. With that reality of truth we can proceed to Live Beyond the Past. The revelation of truth allows us the freedom to make choices. Freedom evolves from truth and truth manufactures choice. If as a child you were reared in a dysfunctional home, you have a choice to free yourself from the guilt of your past and obtain an answer to the question so often asked. Why was I molested? Why was I abused? Why were my parents alcoholics? Why was I put up for adoption? Why was I beaten?

Statistics show that in 1994, over 3 million (3,140,000) children were reported for child abuse and neglect to Children Protective Services (CPS) agencies in the United States.

This figure represents a 4.5% increase over the number of children reported in 1993 (Wiese & Dara 1995). Experts attributed much of the recent 2002 increase in reporting to greater public awareness of and the willingness to report child maltreatment, as well as the changed in how states collect or defined a reportable act of maltreatment. Currently, about 47 out of every 1000 children are reported as victims of child maltreatment. Overall, child abuse reporting levels have increase 63%.

The Statistics are startling and this report did not include those children that were abused and did not report the abuse. You are not alone. Many children are victims of abuse and some were not parented in the ideal American family, where the mother stayed home, cooked, cleaned the house and took care of the children. The father on the other hand, was the breadwinner who financially supported the family.

There are expressed problems in the ideal American family concept. The mother says the father doesn't spend time with the children and family. He comes home and goes to sleep because the twelve-hour work day tired him. The husband says the wife doesn't give him any attention when he comes home from work. The household duties of the mother have resulted in her feeling tired also.

The lack of communication results in the lack of intimacy and can lead to depression, infidelity, anger, resentment and divorce.

Children are innocent victims and suffer emotionally due to the family difficulties. Children grow up and become emotionally unhealthy adults if not given attention, nurture and love. The abused child will grow up to be an adult lacking emotional stability and will seek fulfillment in the abuse of drugs, promiscuous sex, negative relationships, overindulgence in food and other destructive behavior. To include addictive behaviors of food, self-hatred, self-rejection, feelings of unworthiness and shame.

It is important as parents that we have open communication and develop listening skills. This provides an environment where our children feel free to express their feelings, fears, hurts and disappointments. Open dialogue of communication and searching their bedroom could alleviate another Columbine shooting. It's imperative that we maintain open dialogue that allows freedom of expression. It's does not mean that you or I have to agree with your children, however we want to know what is going on with them emotionally.

It would be beneficial once the dysfunction and negative tendencies of your child/ren have been revealed that you pray to break the generational curses from your children, grand children and great grand children.

Psalm 112: 1-3 " Praise ye the Lord, blessed is the man that fearrth the Lord, that delighteth greatly in his commandments. His seed shall be mighty upon earth; the generation of the upright shall be blessed. Wealth and riches shall be in his house and his righteousness endureth forever"

Blessed means that have been empowered to prosper by the love of the universe God.

Proverb 13: 22 " A good man leaveth an inheritance to his children's children and the wealth of the sinner is laid up for the just"

The Generational curses of poverty, alcoholisms, sexual abuse, incest and others can be broken with prayer and counseling. Communication about the family history of dysfunction and abuse should be discussed. Communication is a tool used to express one's individual feelings. You are communicating your feelings about the situation.

In the process of communicating with another adult you need to know that the other person may not change. You are only responsible for expressing your feelings while providing the other individual the choice to accept and/or reject the information. It is important to acknowledge what you want and what you think is right, however, it is not right to impose those thoughts on others.

Conflict is initiated when your mind convinces you that it is imperative that you are right and respected for your opinion and views. Unfortunately this misconception erupts into yelling and anger, which causes a breakdown in communication. In prayer and meditation the love of the universe God will give you the words to say and that will not provoke strife.

If repeated discussions escalate into arguments, the question to ask yourself is, is it imperative that I be right? Evaluate your motives for feeling that you must be right and have the last word at the conclusion of every discussion. Could it be that as a child you were told you are stupid and you can never do anything right? Or as a child your mother or father criticized you about everything that you did or said.

Perhaps, as an adult the mental signals play in your subconscious mind that you must be right and show your abuser that you are right. Blessed are the peacemakers. It is imperative that we become peace seekers and peacemakers.

Keeping peace may mean that you give up your will and humble yourself for peace sake. It would be beneficial if you accept the reality that you are powerless over another human being. The choice has to be made by you to cope with your feelings about other people's choices.

The love of the universe God will give you the strength to control your anger and eliminate provoking words that will generate strife in your relationships. If you apply the principles in this book you will not revert back to using that old negative controlling behavior but use pleasant and desire words.

Manipulation and control are negative methods used to aid a person in getting their way. Some people use sex and money as methods of control. This behavior stems from fear of rejection and abandonment. The manipulator has low self-esteem and the controlling behavior is exhibited in business, personal and platonic relationships.

Adult behavior is learned from childhood experiences, exposures and encounters.

Perhaps in your childhood experience you were made to feel hopeless or someone said negative self-defeating things about you. This behavior is dysfunctional.

Understand that an adult growing up in a dysfunctional home will display unhealthy behavior if counseling is not sought. The adult needs to love and nurture the inner child and allow the child within the freedom to be a child with the control of you the adult.

Past hurts and experiences can ruin your life and inhibit you from having healthy relationships. Make choices today as an adult that you did not have as a child. Choose to live beyond the past. You have a choice to remain in relationships with those who victimized you as a child. You have the choice to remain a victim as an adult. Today, you have choices. We waste tremendous amounts of time struggling with the opinions of others and the need for their approval.

As a result, you find yourselves in relationships and situations that are uncomfortable. The inner child within will give off signals that this is a toxic and unhealthy relationship. In some instances those signals and feelings are ignored and women remain in abusive relationships.

Only later to regret the choice that was made to stay in the relationship. At the conclusion of the relationship these women sing the song "Could have," "Would have", "Should have."

I have counseled many women that were victims of abuse and remained with their abuser. The abuser was always sorry and said " I would never hit you again or I will never say that again". Thereafter, these women stayed in the relationship only later to be killed at the hand of their lover. What does love have to with it?

If you are in an abusive relationship and you feel that he might kill you, if he hit you once, he'll hit you again and the next time he could kill you. Trust those feelings, get out of the relationship and never look back. I suggest that you get counseling.

I believe that we will see an increase of violence, drug use and domestic violence due to the loss of jobs and depression in our country.

For your safety do not negate those feelings. Listen to your inner voice the (Holy Spirit). It could be the right feeling but not the right time to take action. Therefore, develop a financial and personal exit strategy that can be used.

When you are facing life's opportunities to make a decision it can be hard to make those decisions. You can become stuck and immobile when you are unable to make decisions. Don't be afraid to make choices. In the event that you make wrong choices forgive yourself and move on.

Be prepared to make uncomfortable choices. Keep an open mind in the event that the results are not necessarily what you wanted or had hoped.

Therefore, prepare yourself for the lessons in life that will teach you that God is in control, His will is Supreme and He will always do what is best for you.

As we embark on the journey to Live Beyond the Past, remember that life is calling you to walk in the brightness of the truth. In the light of peace your path will be revealed unto you during your darkest hour. God's love and strength will help pull you up to go to the next level, as you follow the guidelines in the book.

The light of truth will reveal inner peace in time. Practice forgiveness of others and yourselves about past mistakes or events. Forgiveness is the fuel that keeps the car running.

When you cherish peace you will forgive other people and yourselves for verbally, physically and mentally abusing you. Eradicate the negative thoughts of your past and the voices of negative people that you allow to make you feel guilty and unworthy.

You can make an individual decision to start the journey to pull yourself up and out of emotional pain and begin to Live Beyond the Past. Allow yourself the choice to be free from the oppressive thoughts, negative self-defeating behavior and the voices that plague your mind.

I recommend that you use these positive affirmations. First, renounce every negative thought that someone has ever said about you. Take 15 minutes a day and look yourself in the mirror and say "I love you and you're special" Love is the only reality and this love affirmation will allow you to see yourself as God sees you and you will see the love in others. This positive affirmation empowers you to make decisions that are based on love, rather than hatred.

Secondly, send positive thoughts and love through prayer to those that you hate. Sending a written letter of love without expectation is another opportunity to sow love where there is strife. Sowing love to others is the initial opening to your soul that allows you to receive love from others.

Next, associate yourself with positive people who have goals and desire to see positive things change in their lives and families. The goals could be personal development, financial, change in attitudes or behavior. If you want to be emotionally and spiritually healthy you must change your environment and associates.

You must separate from unhealthy people if you desire freedom from emotional pain. Separation will allow you to see yourself as God sees you and things differently. Children growing up in dysfunctional homes acquire some unhealthy ideals, thoughts and behaviors. I sure did as I unconsciously mimic the ideals, behavior and thoughts that taking care of others first was more important than taking care of self.

A spiritual awakening allowed me to make the choices necessary to separate myself from unhealthy family members, friends and associates. I learned over the years in counseling and though my personal experiences that people have their individual dysfunctional behavior.

People can only give you what they have received in their life. It is unrealistic to expect love and attention from someone who never received or seen emotional bonding in their family of origin.

People just can't give what they don't have. It is your responsibility to eradicate the old belief system that someone other than you can make you happy. When we make people responsible for our emotions we are rendering our choices and giving them power. The people we invite into our lives should not create happiness but add to our present state of happiness.

Finally, take time to develop a spiritual relationship with God through music, prayer or meditation. I personally enjoy singing spiritual hymns, listening to opera and classical instrumental music that create an environment of peace and serenity.

Meditation is a time of inner thoughts that create peace within. In meditation with the Holy Spirit and God, allows a search of the inner soul. The spiritual evaluation reveals the personal adjustments that are needed. Live Beyond the Past requires that we forgive and have peace with ourselves and then we can give peace to others.

Chapter 6

Successfully Single

There is a battle, Body (the Flesh) versus Spirit: If you are single the love of the universe God wants you to live a victorious successful single life until He sends your mate. This chapter will point to biblical references to help believers live a successful and single life.

The body is the believer's battleground. The Christian life is a struggle of the flesh against the spirit.

In Romans 12:1 the apostle Paul urges that we present our bodies a living sacrifice. Notice that the body is the key area of the Christian's lifelong struggle with the flesh. Much of Paul's message to the Romans is given to the problem.

In Romans 6 Paul explains that legally our old nature was crucified with Christ. But he goes on to command us to reckon (determine) ourselves to be dead to sin. In other words, what I have legally, I do not always live up to experientially. Therefore, I have an obligation to deal with sin personally. That is why Paul goes on to say. Let not sin therefore reign in your mortal body. (v.12). Again, he identifies the body as our major spiritual battleground.

For the believer, the real conflict with the flesh comes down to a decision of the will. If we want to do right, but the body urges us to do wrong, we must spiritually strengthen our wills to say no to the flesh. In this sense, Paul commands us not to yield our physical member as instruments of unrighteousness but to yield yourselves unto God. (v13).

No matter what habit you are struggling with, you can overcome it by yielding yourself to God. Total surrender is the key to total victory. Daily discipline is essential in order to maintain that victory. Do not let up under pressure. Keep up the spiritual fight.

The struggle Paul goes on to describe in Romans 7 is typical of the believer's struggle with the flesh. This is not a description of a lost person, but a saved person. This chapter is not intended as an excuse to live in defeat. It is an honest expression of the struggle every believer experiences. No one is totally victorious all the time. Everyone struggles with the flesh to some degree.

That does not mean you are not really saved. It probably means that you are normal. You are in a spiritual conflict that you cannot win by yourself.

Paul gave three keys to victory in Romans 6 to help us understand how to get over the struggle of Romans 7.

Know. Three times he used the word know (6:3,6, 9). This word means to know deeply or intimately (face to face). There are three things a believer must know in order to overcome the flesh.

Know your position. Verse 3 emphasizes the fact that we are baptized into Jesus Christ. You need to know who you are as a believer. In yourself, you are a sinner, but in Christ, you are a saint. You have been baptized by His sprits into the body of Christ. Secondly, in the symbolism of water baptism, you have been baptized into His death. Therefore, positional, you are in Christ, dead to sin.

Know your potential. Verse 6 emphasizes your potential in Christ. Since your old nature was legally crucified with Christ, you can potentially deny it so that you no longer serve sin. The idea here is not that of "sinless perfection," but of the potential for consistent daily victory in our lives.

Know your power. Verse 9 explains that the believers power comes from the risen Christ who dwells within us. The power to deny the flesh is not merely that of mind over matter. Rather it is God's spirit over our flesh. Since Christ died for our sins and rose again, we have access to His power to conquer the flesh. He can do for us what we cannot do for ourselves.

Reckon. The word means to "depend on" or " place confidence in" something. In Roman 6 Paul uses it as a command. In this sense it expressed faith in action in our lives.

Reckon... yourselves to be dead indeed unto sin (v11) means, "believe it" or "act upon it" In modern English we would say, "You can count on it"!

Dead to sin. The believer still has the potential to sin, but he also has the potential not to sin. Before salvation we were salves to sin and could not resist it. Now we have a new Master, Christ. If we choose to obey Him we can deny our old Master, sin. We are not dead to sin in the sense that we can no longer sin, but in the sense that we have the power to deny sin's dominion over us

Alive to God. The Christian is also to determine by faith that he is spiritually alive in Christ. The born again believer understands that his life is coeternal with the life of God. Because God lives in us by His Spirit we can potentially deal with any problem in life including lifelong habits. You can be free because Christ can set you free.

Yield. The final key to victory over the flesh and it desires is to yield completely to God. We are commanded, *"Let not sin therefore reign in your mortal body" (Romans 6:12)*

We are not to yield to the flesh, but to the power of Christ. Sin can longer dominate us and dictate to us, because Christ is our Master.

Obedience. Behavior that is corrected and instructions followed. When we obey His commands and principles we can expect His blessings in our lives. When we willfully disobey, we will see His blessings withdrawn. The choice is always ours. If you have suffered the consequences of disobedience do not give up. The battle is not over yet. The sooner you turn things around in your life, the sooner you will see His blessings again. No one is ever beyond hope of God's forgiveness or His recovering grace.

Servant of Righteousness. Everybody is serving somebody. You are either living for God, the Devil, yourself or others. You are either serving righteousness or unrighteousness. Every time you choose to do right, you are serving righteousness (see Romans 6:18). When you do what is right once, you help discipline yourself to do right again. Eventually, right living becomes a positive habit pattern in your life.

The battle with the flesh begins in your mind. The scripture says, *"For as the thinketh in his heart, so is he" (Proverb 23:7)* To "think" means to focus your concentration on something specific. Therefore, the Bible tells us to think on these things which are true, good, honest, virtuous and wholesome. (See Philippians 4:8).

Renewing the mind is a continual process of confession and cleansing that focuses our attention on God alone. On the one hand, we must resist temptation, while on the other hand, we are not to be conformed to this world (Romans 12:2) Here Paul has in view the empty world system, which can never satisfy. Turn your mind towards heaven. Do not give in to the world.

BEING SINGLE UNTIL MARRIAGE

To be single means to be "separate" unique and whole. Everyone possesses qualities that are unique to him or her! Your uniqueness must be developed and maintained throughout your life, whether you marry or choose to remain single. In fact, singleness is something that should be pursued before and during marriage because it allows you to maintain your individuality. The key to a satisfying, single life is to love yourself unconditionally and recognize that you are complete and not alone.

To be alone is to be "isolated". God does not want us living isolated, secluded lives, but to exist in close fellowship with Him. Rather than searching for fulfillment through unfruitful relationships, focus on making God your primary companion. In Hosea 2:19, God says we are promised to Him forever and that He will be a partner with us in righteousness, judgement, loving kindness and mercy.

God has personally chosen you to be His! By making Him your Partner and surrounding yourself with other believers, you not only ease the discomfort of loneliness, you also position yourself to experience a fulfilling single life. As you cultivate your relationship with him through prayer and the study of His word, you will become more content with your singleness and inevitably the foundation for a successful marriage!

God has a plan for you, and that plan includes having an intimate, one -on- one relationship with Him. I encourage you to continue building your relationship with God as He prepares you for your mate.

What's wrong with dating?

There are many types of ways of dating, as many as there are people. Perhaps, this is the main problem. Since everyone has a different view of what is right and wrong, there is no standard, no rules, no values, and no right way. I am not saying do not ever date, because there is nothing wrong with it as long as both people set boundaries and remain pure. Then if, standards of excellence are applied and you seek be become acquainted without pretentious games or trying to hide the real you, you will do OK. However, that is not usual date, is it?

The main thing wrong with dating is that we tend to hide from one another. Traditional dating in the US is based on lust, playing games, wearing masks hiding one's true self and seeking what friend and society say. In so doing, you are attempting to keep your date, then girl/boy friend, then fiancé, liking you. Recreational dating is even worse, as it is about self gratification -- seeking fulfillment in someone, or multiple "someone", who cannot possibly meet that need in you, or, it is satisfying your own sinful desires and needs.

Therefore, you never develop a real deep, meaningful or impacting relationship with that person you are dating. So, when you do get married, you will not even know that person. You will only know the perception and idea that you have created for yourself. Then one day, you ask - who is that? And wham! You are disillusioned, and confused, because that person is not who you thought they were. You married an idea, not the mate who was best for you. Thus, you begin a quest to change them in to your idea of what they should be, and, of course, that never works. Consequently, you get frustrated, fed up and end up a shallow, distant relationship or, even worse, in divorce court-- hurt, broken, confused, disillusioned and missing out on Gods wonderful plan!

Consider how dating is a "double standard". In dating, you go from person to person, sometimes several at once, engaging in different forms of intimacy. Yet, when people get married, even in secular society, those various forms of intimacy such as cohabitation, kissing, hugging, sharing emotions, intimate relations, sex and even bringing up children, are recognized as sacred between the husband and wife. In addition, when that trust is betrayed by acting the way we do in dating, the other is deeply hurt and appalled.

The problem is that we learn and practice one way, and all of the sudden we are expected to conform to an entirely different set of criteria. For most people, including Christians, this is too difficult to do. In dating, we assume we are free to participate in the privileges that marriage offers with different partners. This sets up behavioral patterns that most people cannot break.

Then, we are surprised if a married man or woman has an affair, while it is quite acceptable for singles to have a different partner every week, with whom they are physically and emotionally attached. Think about this. If you are giving away pieces of your heart to every Tom, Dick, Rod and Harry/Debbie, Joan and Kate, what will be left for that love of your life? Rampant emotions sexual promiscuity will eat away at you and even remain in you, continually eating away!

When we give ourselves away, the worst consequences are that part may not come back. Even at best, it will diminish us. Dating causes us to be too vulnerable. Most people date like they are married.

They first live together, or act like they are in a marriage, but without the protection of commitment of truly knowing each other! Think this through; you go out, date a stranger you really never get to know, spend a lot of time together, give your hearts to each another- all with no life commitment or covenant!

If you are a child of God, saved by His Grace you have to relax how you speak to the person you will marry. We are His special property! So, until you say, "I do" and give your hearts to each other, beware of who you are in Christ. Because you are God's child, when you engage in inappropriate sexual behaviors, even flirting and kissing, it robs your future spouse and God. This is very dangerous and why most people get hurt after breakup. It becomes an invitation to lose a part of yourself, and steal from God and your spouse - to-be. Consider flirting; you are actually inviting someone else to be attracted to you, to lust after you, when you do not yet belong to each other. You are causing someone else to sin and to desire something that neither you nor he/she can have, something holy, set apart of God!

In dating, there are no Biblical values or precepts included. Then you wonder why you get hurt! In courtship, you are preparing yourself and your future spouse for the covenant of marriage. This is the fortress, the castle that protects, because it is being built brick by brick. The bricks are made of material that builds a real relationship without he superficial mortar that cause the castle to collapse as soon as a rough patch comes alone. Marriage is the boundary that protects your openness and vulnerability. Not convinced? Talk to anyone who just broke up. Sometimes the hurt stay for years or never goes away!

POTENTIAL PROBLEMS OF DATING

- Dating promotes lust and lead to sexual promiscuity.
- Dating promotes a self - centered model of love that is weak and un-Biblical.
- Dating removes the vital friendship and 'getting to know the real person" stage of a relationship.
- Dating promotes a permanent bond between two people who are not meant for each other nor will spend their lives together.
- Dating devalues the real role of intimacy and sex for marriage.
- Dating teaches people to break relationships off when times are difficult, and attitude, which continues into marriage and initiates divorce.

- Dating promotes comparison to what the medic says, un-Biblical and unrealistic standards that few, if any could ever meet. Even the celebrities with all of their money, power, and influence virtually never meet the standards they promote!
- Dating leads to false feelings of intimacy and ignores real commitment.
- Dating promotes an appetite for variety and change, which will create a desire for partner change and discontent in marriage.
- Dating destroys friendships and even church fellowship, leaving Christians alienated from one another.
- Dating confuses a physical relationship with love.
- Dating denies people who know you best to help you out--such as parents and mentors--so you will not a make decisions based on lust, which will not last.
- Dating isolates a couple from other needed relationships, including church and parents.
- Dating distract young adults from their education and preparing for their future.
- Dating creates an artificial environment of evaluating the character of another person.
- Dating will not prepare you for the realities or marriage, as you hide things from each other, denying problems and potential problems until it is too late.
- Dating can cause discontent and rejection of Gods gift of singleness for those who have it.

Okay, you think you have me now! How can we meet our partner without dating? Come on! Do you really think you will meet a good quality person in a bar? In a nightclub, or in a dance hall? I do not want to sound like a prude, as I liked dancing and nightclubs when I was younger, but I would never have considered men there for me nor should you. You have to decide the best environment and situation is in which to come to a decision about someone having the right qualities you desire in a mate. If you think it through, clubs are not it!

So how do you meet someone? (Churches, ministry outings, referrals from family, school, civic classes, study groups, clubs, school, community, hobby, or church based ones friends and friends of friends,) etc, these are excellent places. Look for places where there is no emotional involvement and no agenda where you are forced not to be yourself. Then you can be who you are, and get to know the person as a friend first.

That way you will see the true personality of each other, the behaviors, likes and dislikes. Then you can evaluate how that person acts in a variety of circumstances as they can about you.

You can see if you "click" and have things in common. When you do this before you commence in the relationship, you will be miles ahead and far better off than in the dating game.

So, is dating OK because it is our culture, the way it is? Consider that our culture also says it is OK to sleep around and live together first. So, are you going to follow a corrupt culture, or God's truth? The Bible is clear on how we develop relationships. When we go against God's truth, we set ourselves up for a fall, heartbreak pain, needless suffering, and turmoil!

QUALITIES THAT MAKE HEALTHY RELATIONSHIPS

- Seek a potential mate from quality sources.
- Looks to be first. Build a friendship. This is your first priority and will lay the foundation for the entire relationship! That way, you will get to know each other more deeply and more real!
- They must be a committed Christian; not just saved, but sharing the same theology and spiritual growth aspirations.

- You both need to be growing in the Lord, enjoy going to church, enjoy serving God and others, and be a faithful member of a church.
- You cannot enter into a relationship or marriage in an attempt to fulfill your needs or theirs.
- Be willing to address each other's fault and work them out with God, and a Pastor or counselor.
- Do not rush or be too eager. Allow the relationship to build slowly over months, over years (at least two).
- Always be real, respectful and courteous to your date.
- Do not seek a relationship just to please your family, friends or anyone.
- Be enthusiastic to know more about each other.
- Do not try to court more than one person at a time.
- You must know and/or learn how to resolve conflict and differences without anger.
- Make sure both of you know how money works
- You can not expect a future marriage partner to fulfill your needs in every area. Remember your commitment and covenant to God, that as a Christian, you are holy and set apart for a higher purpose. Remain sexually pure until you get married! If you have committed your heart to God, then it becomes consecrated to Him (Gal 2:20-21).

- Know the type of person that you are looking for in regards to intelligence, personality, goals, spiritual maturity, character, political outlook, future children-- and how to raise them, chemistry (how you click and relate), even appearance be realistic!
- Do not look for someone who is an opposite. They may attract you at first, but some will repel!
- Develop a healthy outlook on what real Biblical love and intimacy is
- Realize that the "dating game" is a dangerous game to play! It will rob you, your future spouse, and God! Whether you are the predator, or the prey, you will be hurt and diminished by the dating scene.
- Listen to your family and to mature mentors whom you trust!
- God calls us to Purity, so be pure!

Chapter 7

Financial Recovery

I've been in numerous financial situations that led to the foreclosure of my home, auto repossession and the filing of Chapter 13 bankruptcy. My financial dilemma began when one income ceased to exist and in my case it was due to separation and later divorce. My husband was the breadwinner.

Thereafter, I had to apply for government assistance for my child and me. During this time I thought I would never recover from my financial troubles. My credit was terrible and I was in debt up to my ears. I couldn't buy anything on credit for years.

My preoccupation with my credit problems created negative thoughts and robbed me of my peace. The pain and despair brought me to tears and then I began to strategize. First, I began to pray and seek spiritual guidance. Secondly, I developed a budget. Finally, I developed discipline in my spending and began to save and invest.

Webster 's Dictionary defines budget as a statement of estimated expenditures, a plan for using resources to finance expenditures. The American Heritage Dictionary defines budget as an itemized summary of probable expenditures and income for given period.

Budgeting in the simplest form is planned spending. A budget is a guide that tells you where you're going and allows you to gauge if you going in the direction that you want to be headed in financially.

You may have ideas, goals and dreams however, if you don't set up guidelines for reaching and measuring your progress, you may end up going so far in the wrong direction unable to get back on track. A budget lets you control your money instead of your money controlling you. A budget can help you meet your saving goals. It includes a mechanism for setting aside money for savings, investments and emergencies.

A budget helps your entire family focus on a common goal. A budget helps you prepare for experiences or large unanticipated expenses that might other wise find you unprepared.

Developing a budget will reveal areas where you are spending too much money and this will help you refocus on your most important goals.

A budget can keep you out of debt or help you get out of debt. The love of the universe God spoke more about money than heaven or hell combined. In the Gospels, (288) in all one out of ten speak directly on the subject of money.

The Bible offers 500 verses on prayer, less than 500 verses on faith, but more than 2,000 verses on money and possessions. God must have realized that managing money and possession would be a problem for most people and therefore, He said and spoke extensive on the subject.

God wants us to learn how to be good stewards over our money and possessions. Jesus dealt with money matters because **MONEY MATTERS!**

The following budgets and charts and examples: These charts and budgets will help you evaluate your financial situation and began to put them in order. If you desire to get out of debt I suggest that you develop a strategy and plan. Debt elimination will not occur as a miracle without a strategy. Miracles don't just happen there must be a strategy developed.

Debt will not disappear without a written plan. Don't spend more money than you make or make more money to spend.

The charts will give you a format to follow and help you on your journey to debt elimination and financial freedom. The word definitions will explain the budget terms.

CHRISTIAN FINANCIAL GOALS INCLUDE THE FOLLOWING:

		MONTHLY	ANNUALLY
1.	TITHES AND OFFERINGS	———	———
2.	FEDERAL INCOME TAX	———	———
3.	STATE INCOME TAX	———	———
4.	SOCIAL SECURITY TAX	———	———
5.	SHELTER	———	———
6.	FOOD	———	———
7.	CLOTHING	———	———
8.	HEALTH	———	———
9.	EDUCATION/DAYCARE	———	———
10.	LIFE INSURANCE	———	———
11.	GIFTS	———	———
12.	TRANSPORTATION	———	———
13.	PERSONAL ALLOWANCES	———	———
14.	VACATIONS	———	———
15.	SAVINGS	———	———
16.	HOUSEHOLD PURCHASES	———	———
17.	DEBT REDUCTION	———	———
18.	SPECIAL CATEGORIES	———	———

*MONTHLY AMT X 12 = ANNUAL AMT

	Monthly Budget Amt	Monthly Actual Amt	Diff/Budget&Actual
Income			
Wages Paid			
Bonuses			
Interest Income			
Capital Gains Income			
Divident Income			
Miscellaneous Income			
Income Subtotal			
Tithes & Offerings 10%+			
Expenses:			
Mortgage or Rent			
Utilities:Gas/Water/Electric			
Cable T.V.			
Telephone			
Home Repairs/Maintenance			
Car Payments			
Gasoline/Oil			
Auto Repairs/Maintenance Fee			
Other Transportation (Bus/Tolls)			
Child Care Auto Insurance			
Home Owners/Rental Insurance			
Computer Expense			
Entertainment/Recreation			
Groceries			
Toiletries, Household Products			
Clothing			
Eating Out			
Gifts/Donations			
Healthcare			
Hobbies			
Magazines/Newspapers			
Federal Income Tax			
State Income Tax			
Social Security - Medicare Tax			
Personal Property Tax			
Pets			
Miscellaneous			
Expenses Total			
Net Income/Income-Expense			

1. **Tithes and Offerings:** all charitable giving – church, United Way, etc.

2. **Federal income tax** – all amounts withheld, estimates paid and any amounts due with tax returns.

3. **State income tax:** all amounts withheld, estimates paid and any amounts due with tax returns.

4. **Social Security tax:** all amounts withheld.

5. **Shelter:** if *renting*, includes rent, heat, lights, telephone, household supplies, appliance repairs, magazine & newspaper subscriptions, and other home-related expenses; if *buying* a home, includes house payments, interest, insurance, real estate taxes, repairs and maintenance, and other items listed under renting.

6. **Food:** grocery store items, papergoods, cleaning supplies, pet foods, including all eating out, carry-out items, and school lunches; also may include entertainment.

7. **Clothing:** purchases, cleaning, repairs, may be divided with a separate budget for each family member.

8. **Health:** health insurance premiums, medical, dental, hospital expenses, drug items, medicines, and cosmetics.

9. **Education:** school supplies, books, lessons, college expenses, uniforms and equipment.

10. **Life insurance:** all premiums, whether paid monthly, quarterly, or annually.

11. **Gifts:** birthdays, anniversaries, special occasions, Christmas, weddings, funerals, office collections, and dues for organizations.

12. **Transportation:** gas, oil, repairs, licenses, personal property tax, and insurance; includes car payments or an amount set aside to purchase your next car.

13. **Personal allowances:** for each family member to spend personally – hair care, recreation, baby-sitting, hobbies, and children allowances.

14. **Vacations:** trips, camps, and weekend outings; trips for weddings, funerals, and family visits.

15. **Savings**: amounts set aside now for future needs.

16. **Household purchases**: major appliances, furniture, carpeting and major home maintenance such as roof and painting.

17. **Short-term debt reduction**: all payments on debt not included in other categories, such as school loans and amounts due to relatives, banks, or others.

18. **Special Categories**: (Caution) anything tailored to your own needs or desires. may include a boat. cabin. airplane or hobby items.

In financial matters God speaks of three Crucial areas: **Ownership, Control** and **Provision**

- **Ownership**- God is the sole owner of everything

To learn to be content, you must recognize that God is the owner of all our possessions.

- **Control** - *I Chronicles 29: 11, 12 "We adore you as being in control of everything. Riches and honor come from you alone and you are the ruler of all mankind; Your hand controls power and might and it is at your discretion that men are made great and given strength."*

- *Provision - Genesis 22:14 God is spoken of as "Jehovah - Jireh " which means "Lord will provide" He takes care of his people and he does not need a booming economy to provide for them.*

Stewardship is key to achieving financial freedom. In scripture the positon of a steward is one of great responsibility. The steward has the supreme authority under his master and has full responsibility for all his masters' possessions, household affairs and raising of children.

Man's only responsibility is to be faithful. It is a requirement of stewards that a man be found faithful. As Christians we have been taught much about giving, but little about how to faithfully handle money.

However, God is not only concerned with the amount that we give, but also with what we do with our entire income. In fact, he is interested in all that we have. By giving a small percentage, many Christians feel that they can bypass all other responsibilities and do as they please with the remainder of their money.

The issue is how to handle faithfully all that God has entrusted to us. The faithful stewards are responsible for what he has whether he has much or little. He can be wasteful and neglectful whether he is poor or wealthy. The way we handle money has eternal spiritual consequences.

Chapter 8

Mortgage Investments

I am a licensed Real Estate Broker and Mortgage Lender. My education and 10 years of experience in finance has equipped me educate families in debt reduction, credit repair, home purchases and secure loans. Empower your self to get a home and turn your mortgage into an investment.

Turn your Mortgage into an Investment

Documentation Check List

- Loan Application
- Picture ID
- Pay stubs for the last 30 days
- Copies of 2 years W2
- If self employed, 1099 for 2 years
- Mortgage coupon or Statement
- Deed on House
- Homeowner Insurance Policy
- Bankruptcy Discharge Letter
- Divorce Decree
- Payoff Notice on bills being paid

WHAT HAS STOPPED YOU FROM BUYING A HOUSE OR REFINANCING?

1) Credit Issues/known or unknown

2) Bankruptcy

3) Foreclosures

4) Liens

5) Judgments

6) Repossessions

7) Late Payments

8) No Credit

9) No Down Payment

10) Fixed Income

11) Disability

12) Social Security

13) Retirement

14) Listening to Others

15) Collections

16) Bad Credit

REASONS TO REFINANCE

CASH OUT

COLLEGE

NEW CAR

RECREATION

VACATION

HOME IMPROVEMENT

START YOUR OWN BUSINESS

REFINANCING YOUR HOME

Have you ever known anyone who had outstanding talents such as?

AUTOMOBILE MECHANICS

A) Engine Mechanic
B) Mufflers
C) Body Repair & Heating
D) Wiring
E) Brakes
F) Air
G) Transmission

CONTRACTORS

A) Painter
B) Plumber
C) Electrician
D) Brick Mason
E) Carpenter

We know there are people who would like to start their own business and don't have the **FINANCE!** **"SO YOU THOUGHT"!**

Here are some of the things **REFINANCING** can do

1) Get Cash
2) Add/ Change A Room
3) Get An Education
4) Buy Appliance
5) Home Improvement
6) Start A Business
7) Buy New Furniture
8) Go On Vacation
9) Payoff Bills

Let's look at this for a minute. You have gotten a credit card at an interest rate of 19%. If you refinance your house, you can pay off the credit card with an interest rate of 6%. How much money have you saved?

For every open account that you pay off, you receive so many points on your credit score, which decreases your interest rate. So let's say you pay off five (5) accounts when you consolidate your bills. You've increase your line of credit and your Beacon Score has gone up, which enables you to receive a better interest rate on your next credit card.

Once your Beacon Score has increased, you will receive the best interest rate available on any of your next purchase.

<u>Landlords</u>

How does refinancing help you?

Tired of repairing the same old things over and over again. It's a known fact that people don't take care for things as if it were theirs. So, why not make the house theirs?

Let me show you how! If your renter has been renting for at least 12 months and you can show a **<u>CANCELLED CHECK OR MONEY ORDER,</u>** you can refinance the house so that they become the owner with no money down and you can get up to 100% of the Appraised Value of the house. This a WIN-WIN Situation.

If they have been renting for more than 12 months, they can buy the house and get cash at closing.

Steps to Financial Freedom

You don't have to be a Millionaire to be Financially Independent
How would you like to have your home paid for, the automobile of your choice paid for, no more punching the clock, enough extra income to pay all of your bills and plenty of money left over to shop and go on vacations whenever you want.

Financial Freedom
Step One:

We can refinance your **_Home_**, take the **_Equity_** (money that you have accumulated over the years) and use it. We have been taught to go to work and make monthly payments on our house until it's paid off, usually in 30 years.

Why are you struggling and you have over $50,000 worth of Equity in your home that you can use **now!** Do you need work done to your home, have you outgrown your home, need a **new car** or maybe you need money to **send your children to college.**

Take a look at this and maybe we can help you understand how your house appraises for **$100,000.**

The payoff of your house is **$60,000.**

We can show you how to do a **Market Analysis** on your property, which is **17%** of the **Appraised Value of your home.** In this scenario, the Appraised Value is $100,000. **17% of $100,000 is $17,000.**

The *Closing Cost* of your loan is normally about 5% of the *Appraised Value.* In this scenario **5% of $100,000 is $5,000.**

Let's subtract our fees and see what we have to do:

House appraised for	$100,000.00
Mortgage payoff	$60,000.00
Market Analysis	$17,000.00
Closing Cost	$5,000.00
Appraisal Fee	$350.00
Credit Report	$65.00

That leaves you with **$17,585** to do whatever you want.

Steps to Financial Freedom

Lets breakdown what we have just established for you.
We have just showed you how to invest your money without coming out of your pocket by refinancing your home and doing a Market Analysis. In five (5) years the Market Analysis, at 17%, will payoff your Mortgage.

Break down

In five (5) years your Loan, at an 8% interest rate, would have paid as follows:
$17,000 Real Estate Market Analysis
$35,220.60 for 60 months (5 years) payment of $587.01
$5,000 Estimated Closing Cost
$350.00 Appraisal Fee
$100 Application Fee
$65 Credit Report

This comes to $57,735.60 total payout in five (5) years.

(Q). Some people have asked, "If I payoff my mortgage in five (5) years isn't there a **prepayment penalty**?

(A). Most prepayment penalties are normally a maximum of five years. So when your mortgage is near payoff, the prepayment penalty date has already expired. Any prepayment penalty for more than five years is for someone with derogatory credit, which sometimes can carry a seven (7) year prepayment penalty. If you should fall into this category, then 1% of the loan amount is charged. So in this scenario of a $100,000 loan, 1% is $1,000, which will be covered in the amount that you've invested in the five (5) years. This will pay your loan off in five (5) years and you will have money left over in your pocket. Now let's make some money.

Next month lets do another Market Analysis. Why? Because the money from the second Market Analysis is all yours. You're only allowed to do one Market Analysis for the Appraised Value of your home, but you can do as many as you can afford without using your Appraised Value. So if you do a Market Analysis every month for a year, in five (5) years you will have earned **$100,000 per month guaranteed** whether you work or not.

Steps to Financial Freedom

Now they become the bank!

The loan for the house they use to live in is **$100,000** and their payments were **$682.13 per month** but now they are going to take **$5,000 down payment** on the property and the monthly payments to them will be **$877.57 a month**. That's a 30-year loan on a **$125,000 house** at 10% interest with no credit check. This house will pay off in **five years** with the Market Analysis. For the next 25 years that payment is, what we call in the mortgage business, **Positive Cash Flow**, and it all goes to them.

What about the other two properties that was bought on the Foreclosure Market?

The two houses that appraised for $80,000 each were paid for with a Market Analysis on them. In five years the CD will mature and they will have $230,000 in cash with no Mortgage to payoff. I advised them to take $3,000 down payment on each property and I will do a 30 Amortization for them. A 30-year loan at 10% will give them a monthly payment of $702.06. The amount of money paid back to them or their children will be $252,741.60 over 30 years. They can either use this paper (CD) to purchase another property without spending a dime, they can sell the paper or even use the paper as collateral. Remember that's two houses.

Lets close it up here. We started with one house and now we have four. The breakdown is as follows:

*$200,000 w/CD pays off in 5 years
*$125,000 w/CD pays off in 5 years
 $ 80,000 w/CD pays off in 5 years
 $ 80,000 w/CD pays off in 5 years

$160,000 in 5 years for the two foreclosed properties.
- **Indicates property that will be paid in full in 5 years**

$200,000 house monthly payments are $1,364.35
$125,000 house monthly payments are $ 682.18

The total monthly payments for all four houses are $2,046.53

$80,000 house monthly payments are $702.06

$$\begin{array}{r} \times 2 \\ \hline \$1.404.12 \end{array}$$

Steps to Financial Freedom
Step Two

We are going to take that extra income per month and **Purchase** some **Foreclosed/Dilapidated Properties** and refurbish them. Why?

To do a Market Analysis on each property.
To show how you can become your own bank.

Let me give you an **example** of a couple that I helped. We refinanced their home, which appraised for **$125,000**. They did not owe anything on their home or property because everything was free and clear. We refinanced the property at **80%**, which was **$100,000**. This is what I did for them:

Market Analysis	$17,000
Closing Cost	$1,000
Brokers Fee	$6,000
Appraisal Fee	$275
Credit Report	$65

Total of all of the above is: $24,340.00.

This left them with a balance of **$75,660 ($100,000 - $24,340)**. I then went to the Courthouse and found **two foreclosed properties** for $30,000 each. I advised them to purchase these properties, which appraised for $80,000 each. So what was our next step? To do a Market Analysis on both properties, which was free and clear.

When you add the balance of monies paid out **($24,340)** to the balance of the two foreclosed properties **($60,000)** you get a total of **$84,340**. Now subtract the new total from the refinance amount. **$100,000 - $84,340 = $15,660**. The couple now has **$15,660** to spend. Now they may have to spend about **$5,000** to paint the houses but that still leaves them with **$10,660** for themselves.

Then I advised them to go find them a new house to live in that's worth at least **$200,000** and we can use the same paper work to purchase that new house for them. It would be nice if they could find a new home on the foreclosure market for about **$125,000** that will appraise for **$200,000**. We could then do a Market Analysis on it. I further advised them that if they could find another house then we could do a **Lease to Purchase Contract**, with the buyer, on the house that they live in now on a 30 year Amortization. Now they own four houses. They have two houses with a Mortgage on them and their new home is estimated at about **$200,000** with payments of **$1,364.35** a month.

There's a profit of **$195.39** from house #2. This profit comes from the $877.57 monthly payments on the $100,000 at an interest rate of 10% subtracted from the $682.18 monthly payments on the $100,000 at an interest rate of 7.25%. Now ad the monthly payments on the two $80,000 (**$1,404.12**) to the profit (**$195.39**) = **$1,599.51**.

$2,046.53 in total payment on Properties
$1,599.51 is total Cash flow on Properties
_____
$447.02 comes out of their pocket every month.

So how much profit are they receiving each month now? Remember after five years the other two houses will be free and clear and they will start to put the money from the other houses in their pocket also.

Keep in mind that they still have their income from before they started to enjoy themselves and they have a new house. We hope that you've learned something here that will bless you and your family for generations to come.

Chapter 9

Debt Elimination

DELIVER US FROM DEBT

DEBT AND FINANCES

YOU ARE TOO GIFTED TO BE BROKE!

The Bible leaves no doubt about God's opinion regarding debt. These two are among the foremost verses that deal with this subject, which is a painful one for millions of people:

Owe no one anything except to love one another, for he who loves another has fulfilled the law (Romans 13:8).

The rich rules over the poor, and the borrower is servant to the lender (Proverbs 22:7).

God does not want His people to be in debt. The only thing we are to owe others is our love, which we are to give freely and in tangible forms. We are to be givers, not borrowers. The price for indebtedness can be high indeed. In ancient times, the children of Israel not only lost much of their land and possessions because of debt that accrued, but some sold themselves or their children into slavery in order to pay their debts.

In Nehemiah 5:3-5 we find a mournful outcry from God's people: There were also some who said, "We have mortgaged our lands and vineyards and houses, that we might buy grain because of the famine." There were also those who said, "We have borrowed money for the king's tax on our lands and vineyards. Yet now our flesh is as the flesh of our brethren, our children as their children; and indeed we are forcing our sons and our daughters to be slaves, and some of our daughters have been brought into slavery. It is not in our power to redeem them, for other men have our lands and vineyards."

This same heart's cry is voiced by a widow who came to the prophet Elisha and said, "Your servant my husband is dead, and you know that your servant feared the LORD. And the creditor is coming to take my two sons to be his slaves" (2 Kings 4:1). The husband of this woman, one of the prophets who was associated with Elisha, apparently had died and left his family in debt. The only recourse that seemed available to the woman was to sell her children into slavery to repay what her husband owed. We may protest, "How horrible! How could a parent sell her children to work off a debt?" And yet that is exactly what we in the United States are doing in strapping our children with a huge national debt. We have gone from being the world's largest creditor nation to debtor status in a matter of only a few decades. What we have done on a national scale we have also done on an individual and family scale. Our children will be forced to pay for our foolishness. God is so opposed to debt that He doesn't even want His people to be the security for another person's debt - in our language today, that might mean being the cosigner on a loan: (*Do not be one of those who shakes hands in a pledge [signifying a loan]. One of those who is surety for debts; If you have nothing with which to pay, Why should he take away your bed from under you? (Proverbs 22:26-27).*) In other words, God doesn't want you to be faced with the possibility of paying another person's debt, a situation that could put your livelihood and possessions into jeopardy - in this case, even your bed!

The Relationship of Debt to Faith

Why is God so opposed to debt for His people? There are a number of reasons. Debt has a negative impact upon the spiritual life. Some of the reasons God is opposed to debt can be discovered when we take a look at the reasons people get into debt:

People get into debt because they buy things they can't afford. When we buy things we can't afford, we are saying to God, "I need this more than I need to be free of debt." We make many credit card purchases so we can bolster self-esteem. We trust in things to give us a sense of identity and well-being rather than trust God for our identity.

Furthermore, when we buy on credit, we aren't trusting God to give us the things we need *in His timing*. We want what we want now. God's plan often requires us to wait for certain things, not only so that we are able to receive them, use them fully, and use them wisely, but also so that others can benefit from God's gifts to us. Trust God for His timing in the blessings you receive. James 1:4 states, "Let patience have its perfect work, that you may be perfect and complete, lacking nothing."

People are in debt because they make unwise investments. God promises to give His people insight, answers, and direction. All we need to do is ask Him for these things, and wait until we are assured of His response. James 1:5-6 advises us, "If any of you lacks wisdom, let him ask of God, who gives to all liberally and without reproach, and it will be given to him. But let him ask in faith, with no doubting." Too few people turn to God to ask His advice about the investments and major purchases they make, such as homes, cars, and other big-ticket items. Others fail to seek God's advice before they enter into partnerships or business opportunities that require them to sign contracts or make financial commitments. I firmly believe that when we ask God for His wisdom, He will give us clear leading about what to avoid and what to pursue. He can see the ending from the beginning, and He knows what will be best for us now and in the future.

People are in debt because they are careless in their purchases, making unwise or unnecessary choices. Much of what we buy we don't need and, in many cases, don't really want six months or a year later. Fashions change. Fads come and go. And although I am not advocating that we be old-fashioned or outdated in our dress or possessions, we should always seek to buy quality items that will last. Again, we need to seek God's wisdom.

People are in debt because they lack forethought for the future. I have met Christian people who believe they are to live in the moment and never have a savings account, much less provide an inheritance for their children. I disagree. The Bible has very positive things to say about inheritance. For example, when Isaac called Jacob and blessed him, he said to him, *May*

God Almighty bless you, and make you fruitful and multiply you . . . That you may inherit the land in which you are a stranger, which God gave to Abraham (Genesis 28:3-4). Further, Proverbs 13:22 declares, "A good man leaves an inheritance to his children's children." Again, a person who lacks forethought for the future leaves no inheritance.

People are in debt because they lose a job or miss work owing to illness or injury. There may be little that you can do to immunize yourself against a job loss, injury, or illness, but if you have saved a portion of your earnings, you are likely to have a financial cushion to see you through hard times. Debt only compounds the pain and emotional trauma that you and your entire family experience when a member of your family is unable to work to help provide for the family's needs. It is easy during times of job loss or serious accident or illness to fall into depression, doubt, or discouragement. You will be less likely to experience these faith - debilitating emotions if you have financial means to pay your bills until you are able to work again. It is far easier to stay out of debt than to get out of debt. Make a decision that you are going to follow God's plan in your finances and that you are not going to fall prey to the alluring messages that tempt you to borrow, buy beyond your means, or spend your money unwisely.

How Much Debt Is Too Much?

How far in debt is too deep?

Much of our society is based upon thirty-, forty-five-, or sixty-day pay cycles. I don't believe that owing a bill for a few days or weeks is tantamount to debt. Debt is financial bondage. You know that you are in debt when you:

> ▢ can't pay bills as they come due.

> ▢ start putting off the payment of one bill in order to pay another.

> ▢ feel pressure regarding your bills.

> ▢ become worried about how you will pay your bills.

> ▢ start looking for quick fixes or quick ways out of your debt.

If you don't feel at ease and confident when you look at your financial situation, you are in debt.

Five process parts for debt Elimination

The process for debt elimination comes without personal evaluation and the education that will bring about our liberation, to glorify God with our dedication and appreciation.

- ➢ **Evaluation**

- ➢ **Education**

- ➢ **Liberation**

- ➢ **Dedication**

- ➢ **Appreciation**

Evaluate your habits

- Your current situation is the result of choices that you made or the effect of events that you were not prepared for.

- We form spending habits that become characteristic which govern our spending behavior.

- Establish where you are and what brought you there.

- **PLAN** to Build
- **STOP** Bleeding
- **START** Healing

Evaluate your monthly expenses

- Find out where you are.
- Add up all the bills paid out on a monthly basis.
- Add the total monthly household income after taxes.

Example of a typical household expenses.

• House payment	$840
• Car payment	$425
• Credit Card (debt)	$400
• Food	$500
• Auto insurance	$250
• Child Care	$360
• Clothing	$150
• Gas	$150
• Utilities	$200
• Other (cable, etc)	$200
Total	$3,475

Annual Income

60,000/Year

$5,000/Month

30%Tax Bracket

$1500/Monthly/Taxes

Income: $5,000
Expenses: $3,475
Taxes: $ 1,500
Potential money left over
$25.00

You still owe ($500) to GOD

If you missed paying tithes you will not be blessed!

- Do we fear creditors more than we fear God?

- Do we pay creditors before we pay God?

New Thought Process

Education:

- How money works.
- How to build economic discipline.
- How to manage debt and become free from financial stress.
- How to build wealth and become financial independent.

Liberation:

- Knowledge of the truth should make you free from the bondage of debt. But only if you are willing to make a change in you're spending behavior.

- Follow God's way of giving (tithes, offering, and ministry).

God said "Freely ye have received, freely you shall give".

LOOK AT WHERE YOU ARE NOW

- Increase your personal net worth.

- Spend more time with your family.

- Open your own business.

- Spend more time with God.

- Have options as to whether your spouse needs to work?

- Provide for your families' needs, including those of your parents.

STEPS TO BUILDING YOUR FINANCIAL SECURITY

- Increase your cash flow
- Manage the debt with a budget
- Create an emergency bank account fund
- Ensure proper protection, (insurance)
- Build long term asset accumulation (401 K, IRA, I Bond)
- Preserve your estate (will)

"Revolving Debt"
The Average American has $20,000 in Credit Card Debt

Based on $20,000 credit card balance @ 18% interest $300 assumes minimum payment of 1 ½%

Payment	Total Interest	Yrs to Payoff
• $300.00	$203,203	62 Yrs
• $301.42	$ 88,500	30 Yrs
• $322.00	$ 38,000	15 Yrs
• $360.00	$ 23,000	10 Yrs
• $508.00	$10,500	5 Yrs

RETIREMENT

• RISING COST OF LIVING:

– Suppose you and your spouse are both 45 years old. Together you earn $100,000.00 a year and you want to retire in 20 years. If inflation averages 4.5% over the next 20 years, you'll need about $176,500 each year to equal your current $100,000 income to maintain the same standard of living.

• RETIREMENT WOES:

– In 2000, older Americans reported a median income of only $13,766. Only 4% of retirees have saved enough and have enough income to achieve financial independence.*

*The 2000 Retirement Confidence Survey, American Savings Education Council, Employee Benefit Research Institute, and Matthew Greenwood & Associates.

DEBT MANAGEMENT AND HEALING

- ➢ Debt reduction starts first with managing where you are.

- ➢ Eliminate unnecessary spending.

- ➢ Separate your wants from your needs.

- ➢ Pray for strength to control your wants.

- ➢ Stop the financial bleeding so you can start healing the debt wound.

- ➢ Stop comparing yourself to what other people have.

Debt Repentance means changing the things that brought us to where we are.

- ➢ Debt humility and financial prayer.

Lord "I want to be a good steward and give more, but I am locked up in DEBT, Lord, I need your help."

> When God blesses and frees you, stand fast in the liberty and be not entangled again with the yoke of bondage and of debt.

AWAKEN

> Document and list all the household debt with monthly pay out totals and payoff balances.

> List the interest rates that you are paying for each interest charge account.

This information is suggested to motivate and inspire you to change your financial direction.

THE AWAKENING PROCESS AND PLAN

> Identify the highest interest-rates and prioritize them going from the highest to the lowest.

> Project how long it would take you to pay off each bill if you stay on your current payment schedule.

> List the bills that can be paid off early.

- Develop and prioritized a plan to help you come out of debt.

- The plan must have weekly, monthly and yearly goals.

- You must develop a realistic weekly/monthly family budget and develop disciple to stick with it.

- Every financial decision must be made to impact the debt elimination and stay on task of the budget.

- Re-evaluate and update the plan and budget as needed.

FREEDOM FROM DEBT

- Pay your tithes.

- Find ways to increase your cash flow.

- Manage your expenses.

- Watch your budget.

- Write down all blessings and debt reduction.

Dedication

- Debt elimination is a process and with dedication to the goal of debt elimination you can be totally debt free. As a man/woman thinketh so is he.

Appreciation

- "Every man according as he purposed in his heart, so let him give; not grudgingly, or of necessity: for God loveth a cheerful giver" You are blessed to have money and you should share what you have.

Chapter 10

Advance In Customer Relations

I developed a Customer Service Training Program and provided training as a consultant for various municipalities, corporations, non-profit agencies, religious organizations and churches. The Department of Education approved the program. The implemented skills will effectively enhance customer service interaction, increase productivity, membership and sales. The objective is to provide customer service skills that will enable staff to demonstrate efficient and courteous human relations skills.

The skills equip staff to handle stress, release frustration harmlessly and adapt to the flexibility of job assignments. I formulated the training to bolster missing skills, enhance customer service interaction and provide excellent customer service. This training promotes enthusiasm, increase job quality, revenue and improves customer interaction. This 4 Phase module is uniquely designed and will effectively increase staff attendance and improve accuracy.

The training provides skills to show employees how they can maintain their job and get promoted in the customer service industry.

Presidents of organizations and corporations contacted me as a consultant and said, "Help, the employees don't know how to speak to people, I'm losing customers and money".

Thereafter, I developed the training with the objective and goal to improve customer service interaction and increase revenue. In the near future, increased revenue and church attendance will be determined on the quality of service the consumer and/or member receives.

4 PHASE CST TRAINING MODULE

Phase I Foundation for Customer Service

♦ Apply your new skills
♦ Attitude of a Customer Servant
♦ You enhance your environment
♦ Control the situation
♦ Verbal Communication
♦ Non-Verbal Communication- Communicates
♦ Body Language Communication
♦ Develop Active Listening Skills

Phase II Caring Customer Service

- Practice perfection
- Develop wholeness
- Your perspective determines response
- Telephone greeting skills
- Know your rights
- Affirmation of abilities/skills
- How to handle face to face encounters
- Role Play

Phase III A Model for Customer Relationships

- Telephone Techniques
- Self assessment before the performance evaluation
- Your presenting self
- Cultural Appreciation
- Separate task from emotions
- Develop a plan
- Conduct periodic assessments
- Acknowledge your weaknesses
- Dismantle myths

Phase IV Creating Positive Outcomes

♦ Don't let your past undermine your future
♦ Behaviors that please the customer
♦ Presenting solutions
♦ How to get what you want and want what you have
♦ Managing Objection
♦ Etiquette's and Manners
♦ Task Orientated
♦ Be a team player
♦ Go along to get along

C A R E

C = Creditability

A= Appearance

R= Responsible

E= Empathy

Be credible

Customers really pay for peace of mind. Customers go back to people, businesses and churches that sincerely want to help. We want sincerity, integrity and the assurance that if there is a problem, it will be promptly handled.

Be attractive

Appearance can be deceiving, but customers and people draw a lot of conclusion about the quality of service on the basis on what they see.

Be responsive

Like it or not we live in an era of instant everything when customers want service, they want it now. Being responsible means being accessible, available and willing to help customers who are having problems.

Be empathic

Every customer is a special individual who wants and is paying to be treated as such. They have unique personalities and wants just as we all do. If you treat them special and solve their problems they will continue to be your customers.

Without question, consistent performance is what customers want most. This means, do what you say you are going to do. Do it when you say you're going to do it. Do it right the first time. Do unto others, as you would have them do unto you.

<u>Customer Service Excellence</u>

This is a list of core beliefs to aid in providing exceptional customer service. These are foundations that you can continuously do what is best for your customer and increase revenue.

1.   Customers are **"valued"** and important people, whether they're in person, on the phone, or by mail.

2.   Customers deserve outstanding service. It is our responsibility to provide service in a manner that is mutually beneficial and with satisfactory results.

3. Customers are not an interruption to our jobs. They are the reason for our jobs.

4. Customers must not feel dependent on us. On the contrary, we are dependent on them.

5. Customers are people like us, not numbers or statistics.

6. Customers are not people to argue, challenge, humiliate, or embarrass. They are to be treated with dignity and respect.

7. Customers have a right to receive prompt and courteous service, regardless of their own behavior.

8. Customers are part of what we do, not people on the "outside."

9. Customers provide us with opportunities to serve them. These opportunities are an outstanding way for each of us to distinguish our organizations and ourselves.

10. Customers have the same expectations we do when we are in the role of the customer being serviced by someone else.

Two groups of words are communicated and expressed in conversations: They are Command and Desire words and the list below are examples of each.

Command Words

- ❖ Have to
- ❖ Got To
- ❖ Expect to
- ❖ Need to
- ❖ Insist
- ❖ Supposed to
- ❖ Obligation to
- ❖ Fault find
- ❖ Want to
- ❖ Blame you
- ❖ You owe
- ❖ Deserve to

Desire Words

- ❖ I would like
- ❖ It would be best
- ❖ I would prefer
- ❖ I would suggest
- ❖ I would rather
- ❖ I would favor
- ❖ I would choose
- ❖ I would select
- ❖ It would be nice

I suggest that you use desire words that will enrich your relationship with others and get more from them.

Conclusion

Pull Yourself Up! Pull Yourself Out! Don't wait on anyone else to do for you what God has empowered you to do yourselves. It's Time for The Next Level!

The lesson of life: I have learned that no matter what happens how bad it seems today, life goes on, and it will be better tomorrow. I've learned that no matter what relationship that you have with your parents, you will miss them when they're gone from your life. I've learned that making a "living" is not the same thing as making "life" I've learned that life gives you a second chance. I've learned that if you purse happiness, it will elude you. But, if you focus on God, your family, your friends, the needs of others, your work and doing the very best that you can, you can find peace of mind and happiness will find you.

I've learned that when I decide something with an open heart and mind, I usually make the right decision. I've learned that even when I have pain that I don't have to be a pain.

I've learned that every day, you should reach out and touch someone. People love and need the human touch of holding hands, a warm hug and a kiss. I have learned that I still have much to learn.

I have dedicated many years of my life in ministry to feeding, sheltering and clothing the homeless and poor. The information contained in the book is taught to empower them and pull them out of spiritual, emotional and financial bondage. Our mission of love gives out clothes and food weekly to the needy. Our vision is to continue to feed the hungry and empower those who are less fortunate. To include providing an alternative to public education by opening charter schools for boys and girls. Your prayers and financial support will help our ministry help others.

The newspaper articles are examples of my work, our Church and its members as we help the poor and homeless in Florida.

City seeks solutions to shelter homeless

TAMPA – Street people flock to volunteer food lines as Tampa officials look to other Florida cities for answers.

By ELIZABETH BETTENDORF
of The Tampa Tribune

The teenage girl with short, matted hair speaks barely above a whisper.

"Could I have a brush?" she asks Pastor Rebba Haley.

Haley was handing out bags of food to the dozens of homeless people who had gathered for a hot lunch Friday under a white tent next to the small steepled church she runs with her husband, Frank. The church sits on a tiny, dead-end street in Sulphur Springs.

Haley, a whirlwind of energy in khaki and sandals, hands her a paper sack filled with a toothbrush, motel soap and shampoo. Then she looks deep into the girl's eyes.

"Do you need something for the baby — talk to me," Haley coaxes.

Tending to the homeless has always been a mission for the Haleys, who run a nondenominational church, day care center and grade school off Nebraska Avenue.

No job is too big.

But in the last few months, the number of homeless showing up on the Haleys' doorstep — and sleeping under the church tent at night — has doubled, creating a much bigger job for the couple.

The Haleys now plan to open a permanent shelter.

Haley blames the problem on the migra-

See HOMELESS, Page 6 ▶

142

com

GARY RINGS/Tribune phot

Pastor Rebba Haley of Living Faith Church serves a hot meal to street people and others in need in the Sulphur Springs neighborhood. City officials are searching for long-term answers for homeless people.

HOMELESS / City looks to S. Florida for ways to fill gap in assistance

◀ From Page 1

tion of homeless away from downtown. That migration, some advocates say, is the result of Tampa's biggest shelter, Metropolitan Ministries, shifting its mission last fall.

The agency shut down its walk-up food line, meaning homeless people must enroll in a long-term residential program to be fed at the Florida Avenue campus.

The move scattered feeding sites among a handful of small churches in central Tampa, like Living Faith, which now feeds about 100 people a day.

It also left some people without a safe place to sleep, homeless advocates say.

The city says it is looking for long-term answers.

In December, Mayor Dick Greco hired a $20,000-a-year consultant, the Rev. Warren Clark, who has been dispatched to talk with social service groups, churches, law enforcement, even the homeless themselves, and patch together a solution.

Tuesday, a delegation of 14 people led by Greco went to Broward County to look at its highly touted program.

The delegation was impressed with Broward's regional homeless assistance centers — in Hollywood, downtown Fort Lauderdale and another in Pompano Beach that hasn't opened.

With walled courtyards, decorative plaster and professional landscaping, the shelters fit seamlessly into their neighborhoods. One even won a beautification award from the local chamber of commerce.

Before Metropolitan Ministries changed its mission, residents of the surrounding Tampa Heights neighborhood groused about litter, vagrancy and homeless men urinating on their lawns.

"Wherever you want to put people, the neighbors complain," Greco says. "It's a big, big problem for everyone in the community, but everyone is trying to help."

Since Fort Lauderdale's 200-bed center for the homeless opened in February 1999, the homeless men, women and families living there have been kept from loitering in the neighborhood. They are kept busy with day jobs, counseling programs, art classes and a fitness center.

No one can simply walk in without a referral. Residents are brought there by social workers, police and others.

"It just looks like a large, attractive building with landscaping," says Steve Werthman, who coordinates Broward County's homeless program.

On a much deeper level, the program is working, Werthman says, because the county has reduced the number of "unsheltered homeless" by 10 percent a year for the last three years.

But news reports in Fort Lauderdale cite statistics showing that about half of the 3,000 people who stayed at the shelter since 1999 may still be on the street.

Fernando Noriega, development administrator for Tampa, says the city's goal is to give street people more than a place to sleep. The city wants to find them jobs and housing, he says.

Haley says that's her goal, too. But something has to be done in the meantime.

She says she is grateful to Metropolitan Ministries for providing food for the feedings at her church. But Haley, a real-estate broker who used to run a shelter for women in Michigan, believes God has called her to give the dozens of homeless showing up at her church each day a place to sleep.

She wants the city or county to donate land.

Friday, the tent was crowded with old women, crying babies and men with vacant stares carrying backpacks.

Haley served meat patties, Spanish rice and carrots. She handed out clothes, blankets and diapers. She gave a jacket to an old woman using a walker.

"It's at our door," Haley says with a sigh. "God knocked and said, 'Here I am.' "

▶ **Elizabeth Bettendorf covers social services and can be reached at (813) 259-7633 or ebettendorf@tampatrib.com**

A church tent has served as a makeshift shelter until recently. The Rev. Rebba Haley posted a sign, right, warning the homeless they cannot stay at night

Homeless forced out of tent

TAMPA – The city tells a neighborhood church the needy can no longer sleep at the makeshift shelter

By ELIZABETH BETTENDORF
of The Tampa Tribune

The Rev. Rebba Haley drops to her knees to face the middle-aged woman with dirty finger nails and sores on her hands.

"The city says you can't sleep here anymore," Haley says, pointing to a large white tent outside the Living Faith Christian Church in Sulphur Springs

The woman, slumped on an old kitchen chair, shakes her shaggy head and looks at Haley with gentle blue eyes When she talks, the words that spill out don't make sense But one sentence is clear:

"I caused you trouble, it's my fault," she says, crying softly in her confusion

Haley cries, too.

"No, no, you didn't cause it, but there's nothing I can do "

Thursday, a sign went up outside the tent where dozens of homeless people eat a hot noon meal and straggle back at night

"There will be no more sleeping under the tent CAUTION If you are caught on church property after 6 p.m you are TRESPASSING," Haley wrote on a sheet of poster board

The sign was her reluctant response to a city inspector's visit giving Haley and her husband, the Rev Frank Haley, one month to clear homeless squatters off her church property at night

The inspector's visit was prompted by a neighbor's complaint The city ended up issuing a warning May 9, saying the couple was operating "an illegal rooming house" out of the tent

Hardly a rooming house, Haley scoffs With dirt floors, folding tables and no running water, it's just a place for dozens of homeless men and women to get out of the violent evening storms and be safe, she says

See TENT, Page 4 ▶

PHIL SHEFFIELD/Tribune photos

Vince Guglielmo, 79, right, and his son Dennis, 47, eat lunch in the tent where the Rev. Rebba Haley of Living Faith Christian Church in Tampa has run a shelter since the fall. They must now find another place to sleep after the city said the church cannot run a "rooming house."

Dianna Brooks prepares a plate to serve those who come for meals, which are provided by Metropolitan Ministries.

GARY RINGS/Tribune file photo

The Rev. Rebba Haley says there are just not enough beds for all of Tampa's homeless.

144

TENT / Homeless must sleep elsewhere

◀ From Page 1

There are 5,744 homeless people in Hillsborough County, according to a count conducted by volunteers this spring But there are only 529 emergency beds, at places such as the Salvation Army, for people who can't find any place to sleep

"Not enough," Haley says Some of those who sleep under her tent once stayed at Metropolitan Ministries Manna House in Tampa Heights The charity closed the emergency shelter and soup kitchen in the fall after it started a long-term residential program and began dispensing free meals at locations across Hillsborough County

Haley's church, Living Faith, has provided the tent for the homeless since the fall. Living Faith is a modest 150-member church tucked off Nebraska Avenue on a dead-end residential street. Church members pick up daily hot meals from Metropolitan Ministries and serve them at noon to the poor. They hand out razors, toothbrushes, combs and soap. Weekly collections pay for an outdoor portable toilet, GED classes and substance abuse counseling

"We're very grateful to Metropolitan Ministries for the food, and we're doing everything we can to move the homeless to self sufficiency," Haley says

"We just need more help."

Haley, who sits on the Hillsborough County Homeless Coalition, appealed to Mayor Dick Greco for that help last month She met with him for two hours.

Greco says he plans to tour the tent and church sometime soon, but that he can't offer an immediate solution

"I reminded her that she has neighbors and that they have a right not to have 20, 30 or 50 people living in a tent across the

PHIL SHEFFIELD/Tribune photo

Since the fall, dozens of homeless people have come to the tent in Sulphur Springs where they sleep on the dirt or on folding tables. Some of them say, despite the conditions, it's still safer than other places.

street," says Greco, who has been looking for ways to deal with homeless people across Tampa

"She's doing a very good thing, and we're doing our best to find another location," Greco says

Cynthia Miller, the city's director of intergovernmental relations who studies homeless issues, says outreach workers from local social service agencies plan to visit the street people who have been relying on the tent for shelter

"We've talked with Pastor Haley and understand she is trying to do God's work, but these people need an appropriate place to sleep," Miller says

Haley admits that the tent is less than ideal, but the people who use it have few alternatives Many are severely mentally ill. She prays someone will donate a building big enough to house a shelter, showers and a soup kitchen

"We don't have air conditioning, we don't have a bathtub and it's hot in there — sometimes 100 degrees," she says of the tent, pitched under a cluster of shade trees "People are sleeping on the ground and folding tables "

Dennis Guglielmo came to the tent Monday He pulls the back seat out of his 1985 Chrysler Voyager so his 72-year-old father,

Vince, can sleep in the safety of the truck Dennis then stretches out on the car seat on the ground inside the tent

Vince, who drove an oil truck for 30 years, was robbed and stabbed in the hand a few weeks ago by thugs in the hallway of the rooming house where he was staying He rubs the scars on his bony hand.

"He's all I've got," Dennis said of his father "And this is a lot safer than sleeping on the streets "

▶ **Elizabeth Bettendorf covers social services and can be reached at (813) 259-7633 or ebettendorf@tampatrib com**

145

About the Author: Dr. Haley teaches in Florida colleges and public schools. Reba received her Master of Science Degree in Psychology and Doctoral Degree in Counseling from St. Thomas Christian College in Jacksonville, Florida.

She is a certified and licensed Clinical Licensed Counselor with the National Christian Counselors Association. She is a financial consultant, licensed Real Estate Broker and Mortgage Lender. She is a consultant, corporate trainer and grant writer for local government, municipalities, churches, civic groups, not for profit and profit organizations.

She is a motivational speaker, lecturer, author and member of the National Speakers Association. Her hobby is music. She released her first gospel CD in 1997 "Are You Ready For The King" She also in 2002 released " Jesus Cover Us With Love" and recently released her new CD in June 2003 "Who Do I Call? I Call On Jesus."

Visit **www.RebaHaley**.com